WHERE THE WANTING LEADS US:
READING THE POETRY OF NORMAN FINKELSTEIN

Table of Contents

Midrash

Henry Weinfield, Peter O'Leary, Mark Scroggins, Michael Heller,
Ariel Resnikoff, Eric Selinger, Maeera Shreiber

Reviews

Introduction

This volume brings together a range of writing from various contributors, seeking to celebrate through examination the literary achievement of Norman Finkelstein. Widely regarded as one of the major scholar-poets of his generation, Finkelstein has crafted a singular poetics, sensitive to the overlapping traditions of Jewish mysticism, radical poetics and post-modern thought. Taken together, these sources resonate within Finkelstein's body of work as a profound record of human yearning. *Where the Wanting Leads Us* features a series of scholarly essays that address themes central to the poet's seven full-length collections of poetry, from the exile's construction of visionary community to the poet's restless pursuit of world in word. The volume also includes a previously unpublished interview and a midrashic annotated commentary of a section from the poet's long poem *Track*. *Where the Wanting Leads Us* intends to provide an introduction to Finkelstein's work for the unfamiliar reader as well as a critical resource for the already conversant.

—*J. Peter Moore*

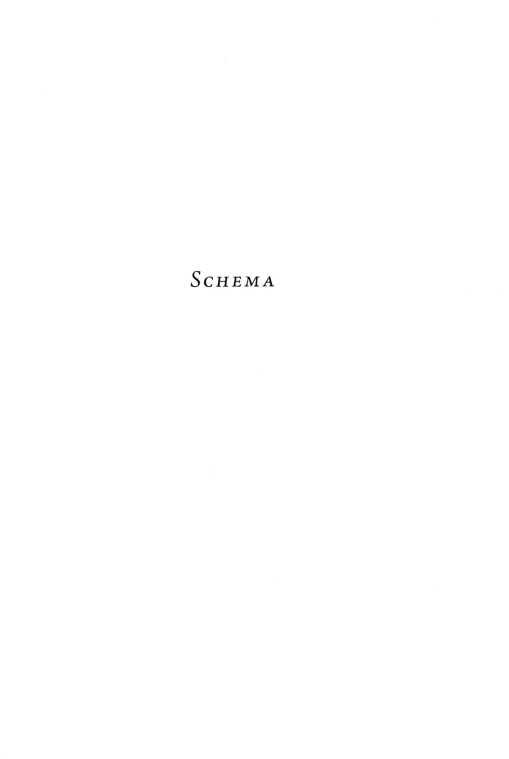

SCHEMA

Beyond "the marketplace of the feasible": tracing Norman Finkelstein's poetic oeuvre to its source and sustenance in his 1977 debut, *The Objects in Your Life*

Kristen Renzi

It's fitting that Norman Finkelstein's first book of poetry, *The Objects in Your Life* (House of Keys, 1977), opens with an unnamed poem, marked instead by the quotation-captured repetition of its first line: "because we return to the scene of death" (1). Ironically fitting, of course, because this opening salvo in a career full of poetry books to come is so insistently backward looking, even at the moment of its inception. After all, as a scholar of poetry alongside and inside of his own poetic creations, this continuous return to voices, lives, experiences long lost (a kind of death, sure) populates many of Finkelstein's later works. But this first title/first line, in its meld of birth and death, is also, strangely, arresting. This death scene we return to, "not once, but many times," is one that transcends the ordinary boundaries of time, lodging us in an insistent present in which "the sands of the hours of implacable night/ are forever inverted" (3–4). In this topsy-turvy world of perpetual hour-glass flipping, we encounter an otherworldly space less Bakhtinian carnivale and more anti-gravity simulation at your local fair: vomit-inducing, sure, but also perspective-altering, particularly if there is no way to get off the ride.[1] This otherworldly scene is not mere rebellion, nor simple mourning, nor pure madness: it is the shadowland of poetry.

---

1. See Mikhail Bakhtin's work, *Rabelais and His World*, from *The Bakhtin Reader*.

This poetic shadowland—that is, Finkelstein's particular version of the shadowland all poets and critics of poetry engage in their own ways—is something I have come to know from multiple directions. To acknowledge that I know Finkelstein not merely through his words on the page, but also through his words in person—that I know him as a poet and a critic, as a colleague and mentor, and as a friend—is not, I hope, to cast suspicion upon the words I write here, nor is it to merely stake out a space for biases and investments. All critical enterprises come with their own limitations and qualifications of what it is to "know" the writer-object of their study, and it is not clear that a personal friendship with an author would either strengthen or weaken one's ability to comment on their work—it merely conditions it. No, my point in raising your, my reader's, attention to these multiple fronts through which I've come to understand Finkelstein's verse is to better chart the course through which I encounter *The Objects in Your Life* and the poetic shadowland it introduces: that is, through the opposite temporal end of the spectrum, and through another evocation of poetry's special relationship to the real—*The Ratio of Reason to Magic*.

What is *The Ratio of Reason to Magic*? Of course, in one sense, it is the collection of new and selected poems by Dr. Norman Finkelstein, published in 2016. As such, it is the occasion of my first encounter with (some of) *The Objects in Your Life*, as select pieces from this original collection occupy the first pages of *Ratio*. It is also, literally, a fragment of a line from "Ratio," one of the poems from Finkelstein's more recent individual poetry collection, *Inside the Ghost Factory* (2010).[2] But this question is also, I would suggest, one that haunts the pages of Finkelstein's poetry from the very beginning: haunts them *because* solving such poetic math is both impossible and made possible by poetry, *because* poetry itself is rendered, in Finkelstein's care, nothing if not an echo-chamber of other hauntings, and *because* this haunted thing, poetry, is (so often) both the form and content of Finkelstein's verse. "This rhyme," claims Finkelstein's "Ratio," "measures the ratio of reason to magic./ Every break indicates that something has/ slipped through" (7, 8–10). This fascinating configuration of rhyme as a device

2. Quoted from Finkelstein's collection, *The Ratio of Reason to Magic*, page 278.

WHERE THE WANTING LEADS US

that measures a mathematical relationship between two central poles of what, to me, make poetry both a frustration and a joy to encounter—one made of reason, logic, and one of expansive, strange, and ineluctable magic—anchors Finkelstein's work throughout his almost 40-year career of poetic engagement. Like Freud's "dreamwork", the poetic "break"—both in terms of the breaks in individual lines and the break from the world as we know it that the ratio-ed magic of poetry is—allows for the entry of the otherwise repressed, ignored, or rejected into our mindscape.[3] As Finkelstein's speaker in "La Quinta Del Sordo," the third poem in *Objects*, would phrase it, this break or "open wound/ gapes wide enough to hold the world" (1–2). Indeed, the speaker begins this poem by pronouncing the crucial importance of such poetry-work: "it means everything, to think/ the thoughts that must remain unsaid" (1, 3–4). This tension between engaging the unsayable thoughts and thinking at all, here illuminated by the line break, is a radical argument that poetry must remain present in our lives: it is this object, indeed, that enables that crucial verb "to think" at all.

And yet understanding and indeed embracing the distinction between a traditional mode of thinking, with an emphasis on reason and logic, and the alternative mode of thought to which a space like dreams, like poetry, provides access is key for Finkelstein's speakers in *Objects*. In the second section of "From a Vatic Landscape," for instance, the imperative voice of the poem warns us readers to heed the potential treachery of the voices, the loves, and the fictions that deceive: we're cautioned that such "deception/ is no small matter" (16–17). And yet, in such a case, the dreamers have the advantage over those who engage only in the realm of thinking; we hear that while "the thinker is led / astray by such conjectures," the dreamer is able to "drea[m] on, assuming / the world" (19–20). What might be construed as merely a power to ignore on the dreamer's part, making the advantage of this position perhaps emotionally enticing but intellectually questionable, is immediately challenged by the ending claim that finishes the poem's twentieth, and final, line: "the dream reifies the world" (20). It is the dreamer's power that makes real the world, not the thinker's; indeed, in

---

3. See Freud, *On Dreams*, 16.

this cosmology, the thinker is bewildered, while the dreamer can, if not understand the world, at least create it.

Yet the final, fifth section of this same poem construes this relationship between dreaming and thinking differently, flipping the ascendency and the relationship between reality and dreams once again; it reads, "of the world and the dream, / this much is known: that they exist as a / paradox, bounded by thought" (3–5). Here, thinking becomes a way to join, if not resolve, the paradoxical relationship between dreams and reality, in which dreams both seem outside of and constitutive of this reality. The term "paradox" is especially apt here: the prophecy or "vatic" nature of this poem seems less keyed toward any clear conceptualization of the relationship between these ideas of thought, dreams, and reality and more toward the insistent claim *to* their relationship. Put differently: the ratio of reason to magic, it seems, is not one that has a clear numerical value to fall back upon. What seems sure, for Finkelstein, is merely that there *is* a ratio that puts them in relation.

In what follows, then, I will look closely at *The Objects in Your Life* in order to outline some of what Finkelstein's poetry allows us to engage with mentally, emotionally, physically through this ratio/ relation: both the things that we think we should think about and those that we keenly feel the taboo against our thinking. Finkelstein's body of work, both critically and poetically, has been, to varying degrees, concerned with this enterprise of thinking the unthinkable. The lineage of Jewish poetry that Finkelstein both works within and also writes of in his critical collection *Not One of Them in Place* (2001), for example, focuses somewhat idiosyncratically on writers whose aesthetic stylings, with their modernist bent, prove to be challenging to read and think through. As Mark Scroggins notes in his review of this book, Finkelstein's reading preferences tend to embrace the Objectivist tradition, a school of poetry that, in Scroggins' words, is devoted to creating "spare, taut, free-verse artifact" that is "the antithesis of the Romantic lyric" (127). And yet this is but one side of Finkelstein's intellectual investment; as Romana Huk writes in reference to another of his critical endeavors published less than a decade after *Not One of Them in Place*, he manages to yoke together what would, a mere "dozen years ago" have been "all but unthinkable": the "field of radical poetics" and the "sacred" (225). In this collection, *On Mount Vision*, Finkelstein's attraction to, if not the Romantic lyric, then certainly the sublime impulse is on full display. This commingling of the modernist formal experiment with the transcendental power of language can be found in Finkelstein's poetry itself, particularly as it circles around the mysteries of thought/unthinking, as well as the tenuous, always partial, unveilings poetic verse provides to these mysteries. There is something to be uncovered through the project of a poem, *The Objects in Your Life* seems to say, which can be made use of, if only we are willing to undertake the work, and the journey, to find it.

"Alone, Alone, All All Alone"[4]

Finkelstein's speaker opens *The Objects in Your Life*, and the poetic oeuvre it ushers in, with a "fabulous quest" (as all proper literary heroes do), replete with "forests and rivers and wild beasts" (20, 21). Later, through the allusion Finkelstein makes to the German Renaissance painter Matthais Grunewald's painting *The Temptation of St. Anthony*, the speaker's quest away from the scene of death is aligned with the hermit Anthony's own journey to seek another, better hermit, suggesting the quester's grail might be either a better version of himself or a true interlocutor/partner beyond the memories of the dead. Step one, however, is the speaker's dawning realization that he is actually in this "scene of death" in the first place, and then must go on a quest, at all (1). After all, the speaker has, until recently, been under the now-absurd impression that he was "not alone" (16); upon discovering he has actually been in and among the dead at a "table of sweet perdition," accompanied only by "columns of smoke" that "denoted absence," our speaker wonders at his own previous credulity (12, 18, 19). Our hero has not exactly been asleep (he's dead, remember!), but rather held back from acknowledging his true state through "the weight of material circumstance" (15). Here, he struggles not with the fantastic dream-

---

4. From Coleridge, Samuel Taylor, "The Rime of the Ancient Mariner."

state of a darkly-inflected Rip Van Winkle-esque nightmare but the sleep that plagued the generation following Irving's: the people's false consciousness.[5]

What strikes me, in this imagery, is the sense of aloneness that this speaker, like those questors of literary yore, embodies, even when he does think himself in company. Like a Van Winkle out of step with his time, or an Odysseus-esque wanderer who becomes "vagabond, given to no homestead," the speakers of many of Finkelstein's poems are individuals in touch with their ultimate isolation ("From a Vatic Landscape," section 5, 19). The pull between the individual and the sense of community from which they are estranged is most clearly pronounced in the opening vision of "Chance," a rare Finkelsteinian prose poem made up a series of vignettes, the first of which reads as follows: "my friends stand behind a fence. They are mad. They need / me and I am kept from them" (1–2). Whether these fellows are insane or angry, the speaker's frustration at his impotence is emphasized by the lineation break after need. The barrier the speaker is held back by is, painfully, not one of ignorance. So, too, the vision in the final vignette of the poem, which features a community of female weavers, who are figured by Finkelstein as, simultaneously, "ancestors," "products of [the speaker's] dreams," and "housewives living in Pittsburgh with homes and families and secrets that [the speaker] shall never know" (28, 28, 29–30). In the poem's final lines, when the speaker recognizes that "[he] is one of" these "weavers of disparate elements" on these trans-temporal looms, our wanderer becomes less Odysseus and more Penelope, the one left waiting at home.[6] By manifesting both halves of the traditional questing pair—the male adventurer and the steadfast woman to whom he'll return—this poem further isolates the speaker, even as it suggests the speaker's duality amid individuality. These poems draw no simple romantic yearning on the part of the speakers for their other halves; instead the speaker's attempts at love and connection are fraught with the acknowledgement of the fragile treachery of love, in which the speaker's own estrangement from himself is related to the challenges

---

5. See Washington Irving's short story, "Rip Van Winkle."
6. See Homer's *The Odyssey*, Book 2.

connection pose. Which does not make it any the less of a goal for the speaker to find—it just qualifies the celebration of achieving it.

For instance, while questing, our speaker-cum-hero of ["Because we return to the scene of death"] encounters obstacles that remind him of his ultimate isolation not only from his community but also, interestingly, from himself. When joining a group of similar questers at the close of day in protective, torch-lit companionship, their circle of camaraderie is broken by their own possessions, "mirrors" that they "h[eld] before" themselves until they "cracked remorselessly" (24, 24, 25). Later, our speaker is confronted with another warped reflection of himself in the form of a group of men "chained/ to dogs and to each other with fetters of glass," whose stares back at him mirror his own "death's head smile" (61–62, 63). The glass that binds, the mirrors that intercede, and the dogs that follow: these are temptations that our quester, like Saint Anthony before him, must resist. And yet the tools of his resistance are not supernatural, as in Anthony's tale, but the very human combination of "poems/ and unborn children" (59–60). With these two implements alone, it seems, our speaker is asked to respond to the chained men's demand: "we must raise the stinking corpse of love/ and sing and sing and sing" (68–69).

"Because it is bitter, / And because it is my heart"[7]

Poetry, then, and love song: progeny of the poet, born out of the afterlife of the already dead, this vocalization from the gravesite constitutes this particular shadowland of poetry, which is both extra-worldly and worldly-tether. The speaker, the poet, exists as mirror of and yet distinct from other men, and in Finkelstein's oddly present-tensed idyll, constitutes a simultaneous prophet and historian of the damned. This is not a hopeful debut poem in any commonsensical sense of the term. And even a quick peek at the table of contents of the collection will clarify that it is in good company: the trickster-cum-masked devil-clown "The Harlequin," for instance anchors the book's sparse fourth poem, while "Entropy," "Failing Light" and "A Call to the Bones of Men"

7. See Stephen Crane's "In a Desert," from *The Oxford Book of American Poetry.*

are subsequent titles in the collection. Perhaps the most ominous, "How It Ends," casts an apocalyptic cloud over any of the soothsaying that "From a Vatic Landscape" might portend. And yet we also have love: explicit in the seventh poem's title, implicit in the dedication to another, and punctuating various other pieces throughout the collection, this "stinking corpse" is indeed raised, and praised, in song throughout Finkelstein's work, not, perhaps, as antidote or redemption, but certainly as palliation.

Toward the middle of collection, for instance, Finkelstein places a poem entitled "The Centuries of Love" that engages the ironically generative and killing power of love. The poem opens with the pessimistic contradiction: "the centuries of love/ are killed by their own creation," which, through the course of the piece, comes full circle to the seemingly opposite ironic truth: that "love will never quench/ the fire of love" (1–2, 25–26). A few lines before this circular ending, the speaker most clearly asserts the duality of love: "in time love brings to ruin all things/ And nurtures them back to health" (21–22). This portrait of love as both destroyer and mender can skew redemptive or devilish— it reminds me simultaneously of the forward-thinking powers of forgiveness and of the serial killing torturer who repeatedly holds victims underwater to the point of consciousness loss, then resuscitates them only to dunk them anew after the recovery. These life-filled yet destructive images of love continue: in "Actuating the Vast," the speaker can only muster the following about love: "it too is strained, loses/ what little effect it had" (18–19). And yet in this same poem, despite the following nihilistic rephrasing of the above depressing statement about love ("in a word, there is nothing" (19)), the speaker still engages a small hope in such darkness: that he might "touch the fire/ and not be burned" (41–42). To this speaker, as with other speakers in this collection, love is powerful not because of its origin outside the speaker, but rather because it is a creation of the speaker through which he attempts to maintain a sense of humanity—humanity defined here by a state of both knowing and yearning. Despite (or because of) the state being "human," which the speaker claims causes us to "suffer the brunt of cognizance," the human being also is "held" (on earth, to sanity, like a lover) by a "tendency to call/ things into being" that "was a passion" in them (26, 27, 35, 32–33, 34) And in the following poem, "A Call to the Bones of Men," we hear that "the heart/ is a careening planet" (23–24). In these pieces, the mess of optimism and pessimism becomes, simply, realistic. Love may be no sure antidote—indeed, it may be the poison that causes the need for such antidote in the first place—and yet it calls us, surely.

Nowhere is this duality of love more poignantly expressed than in the poem "Orion," which Finkelstein dedicated to his first wife, Kathy. Though the poet's own personal experiences of the vicissitudes of married love would unfold in future decades, this poem is remarkable for its honest engagement with the plight of the jaded lover who cannot but hope, despite oneself. The poem begins with a kind of forecast: "Our bodies change./ They know beforehand/ of what is to come" (1–3). What future knowledge such a change either heralds or responds to is not made clear, but love's traditional yoking with constancy renders the whiff of change at least suspect, if not ominous. In a set of paired couplets toward the poem's center, Finkelstein gracefully expresses this knowing love. He writes:

> It is such
> That we should never hope.
>
> But on a winter's night
> it is enough.

The fragility of these lines, alongside their courage, bespeaks a worldliness beyond the poet's own years. Indeed, these spare words capture well the pessimistic hope that characterizes the volume, and a mature sense of love that many poets and speakers grow into, rather than express at the outset. To see this sentiment so early in Finkelstein's career need not, however, demark a precociousness—rather, I'd suggest that at least some of these speakers' willingness to enter into love's hazards open-eyed comes from their engagement with another aspect of life's inevitabilities that most of us mortals put off as long as we can—our mortality.

11

"Death is a Dialogue between"[8]

Finkelstein's poetic shadowland is populated by ghosts, which is no hyperbole. The collection begins, as mentioned above, by not only coming upon but rather "return[ing] to" the scene of death (1). Thus, even as the poetry collection opens, we are greeted by a speaker whose familiarity with the land of the dead is highlighted. These dead are not only the speakers' literal ancestors (as in "Chance") but also the poet's artistic ones, harmonies and echoes that, I hope, not only the above paragraphs but also the section titles I've given to this paper indicate. Though such echoes of poets from past centuries—Coleridge, Crane, Dickinson—may be my own throughlines I chart between Finkelstein's debut and the English-language poetic inheritance we both draw (in part) on, I find these to be helpful touchstones in mapping out the curiously unwavering stare Finkelstein's speakers employ toward their own mortality. With this familiarity comes not only a kind of ease but even a welcoming attitude toward death. In "La Quinta Del Sordo," the speaker likens himself to Job, eternal sufferer of the Biblical Old Testament. His pain is so acute that the speaker yearns "to be released! / To be free of the tension,/ the slow, forceful weight and the pain / of breathing" (21–22). And yet, to be released into death, pleasant though that may seem in theory, is neither Job's lot nor the speaker's. Instead, rather than fighting the "stunning blow" that seems to take one's breath away, only to return it in that damn torturous pattern of love (above), the speaker ultimately urges himself to "accept, accept/ and reaffirm. And seek for steady ground" (44, 47–48).

The human project of remaining surefooted among ruin, suffering, death, and pain might, ironically, be one of the anchoring grounds of this book. What might at first seem a sort of superhuman detachment from the ills of the flesh with which "La Quinta Del Sordo" ends is not, in fact, one of imperviousness. In the poem most explicitly about the end of life, "How it Ends," our speaker figures death, this time, as not welcome but as monstrous, coming at him with "mammoth jaws" (1). Despite life's pain, which is not unique to the speaker (he feels,

---

8. See Emily Dickinson's poem with this opening line.

after all, merely "the plain ache / of common bird-song" (17–18)), he cannot bring himself to depart "this sad country," instead feeling "bidden to stay" (21, 22). The question this tension develops into, "how do we suddenly leave off living?," is a remarkably tender expression of death via the trailing alliteration of "leave off living", even as it marks the violence of the rupture through the word "suddenly" (23). The death that circles throughout this book remains in marked contrast to this end of life denoted above—indeed, one might suggest that through haunting, through return, through impossible paradoxes, the notion of death that this book charts is much more omnipresent, and thus much less final, than a sudden cutting off.

The final poem in the collection, "The Objects in Your Life," makes clear the razor's edge that we all walk between death and life, illusion and illumination, hope and despair. The poem's opening stanza begins with the claim, "the objects in your life sustain your delusions" (1). The means by which this work is completed is elaborated by the speaker in the remainder of the stanza: we learn that these objects "create a path of least resistance, / a tenuous bridge" of thought that provides safe passage of the obedient thinker across "the abyss" below (2–3, 4). Yet this safe passage is bought, in part, by ignorance: the thinker is "unaware of the abyss" and blind to boot; "without recourse to sight," we hear, one's thoughts "do not know / 'the open air'" (4, 5, 5–6). In this strange figuration, thoughts are like always-caged birds whose very survival is conditioned by their surrender of a freedom they've never known the cost of surrendering. And yet, in order to represent this, the speaker of this poem must have a (forgive me!) birds-eye-view, the perspective of those real, free-flying birds, who can see the fettered nature of the safety enjoyed by the thinker, even as it also can see the true danger of the abyss below.

Perhaps it is unhelpful to say that the speaker of this poem has the dubious misfortune of sighted awareness, or that the abyss and its ruin is welcomed by the poem's final image. Our questor from the opening poem here, at the collection's end, finally reaches the quest's physical and psychic endpoint:

> When you finally come within sight,
> when the ruined chateau again is repaired,
> when it is past midnight and the guests are tired,
> the musicians fatigued and the servants bored,
> what young woman is dancing, light and airy,
> before the astonished multitude? (25–30)

As the speaker enters into awareness and "comes within" the realm of sight, the vision before him is of a ruin restored, a party long underway, and a single other still enjoying the festivities despite the late hour. It is not clear in this moment if the speaker has fallen into or has moved safely beyond the abyss; it probably doesn't matter which one. The poem's final stanza concludes with an image the mixes birth and death imagery until the two are indistinguishable. The speaker narrates the experience as follows: "The objects in your life are falling away. / In beautiful patterns, they pass before your eyes, / and you are blissfully deserted, as naked as a star" (35–37). It's difficult to know how to read such an awakening; its transcendent tone is one of deliverance and rebirth (things are "falling away," the speaker is rendered "naked"). Yet it also bespeaks an ending: the speaker is "deserted" at the ending of the poem (certainly of worldly possessions, if not of human companionship). There is one last dancing guest at the party, the woman who, "mad with delight," is neither a clear balm nor certain damnation (33). We have learned, as readers of the text, to both never trust and to ultimately trust love—and thus in the final images of the book, we are left pondering the closing thoughts of a speaker who has either been awakened into full cognizance of reality or who has finally (or yet again) given up the ghost. Perhaps the greatest gift that this poem, and this collection, can give us is the question, rather than the certainty, of which to choose. As a more explicit reference to a poetic legacy in "La Quinta Del Sordo" makes clear, it is perhaps only in the guise of the fool that one can hope for something as absurd as "a faithful love" in the topsy-turvy, counterintuitive, nay apocalyptic world we inhabit (Yeats, "The Fool by the Roadside" 12).

*

It's an odd thing to be, a lover of words, of life, particularly in the face of darkness and death. Throughout Finkelstein's entire body of work, one confronts these confounding juxtapositions. In the debut collection explored above, three distinct strands of Finkelstein's poetic investments within this (and other, future) collections emerge: the relationship each of us has to our own alone-ness, to our heart's own complex desire for love despite pain, and to our past, mortality, and the concept of death more broadly. Explicit mention of the work that poetry does in drawing out these relationships' particular contours and limitations weaves throughout the book. As such, *The Objects in Your Life* exerts both meta and prophetic force. Finkelstein's poetry, here and in his larger oeuvre, alternates between a romantic's sensibility toward the sublime and an experimental writer's sense of obstruction and limit. His immense work *Track*, for instance, plays with compression in both its design (according to strict numerical limitations) and its elliptical meditation upon words:

> *Translation:* you may no longer
> write this way
>
> *Or:* you may no longer
> go this way
>
> Those of you
> awaiting translation
>
> Right
> this way[9]

This structural play may seem at odds with the lyric sensibility of something like "what do the stars / care about man? / Only that he make their light / the subject of his song," and yet the focus of both— the fragile connections between words and beings we honor and break each day—remains constant (["Because we return to the scene of death"] 37–40). Finkelstein's first book, in its attention to the "break,"

---

9. Quoted from Finkelstein's collection, *The Ratio of Reason to Magic*, page 172.

the porous nature of poetry that marks absence through its very being, sets the stage for a career-length fascination with what the poetic line can and cannot mark out, along with the magic and sense found therein. I've highlighted, I hope, not only the strains of engagement with paradox that Finkelstein embeds throughout his first collection's treatment of loneliness, mature love, and mortality, but also the richness that his poetry suggests can be found by leaving this paradox intact. As Auden, in "In Praise of Limestone," finds a home for us, "the inconstant ones" amid porosity, so too does Finkelstein's poetry, which (like lace) is beautiful by virtue of both its material and the space around it (1).[10]

Works Cited:

Auden, W. H. "In Praise of Limestone." *The Norton Anthology of Modern and Contemporary Poetry*. Ed. Jahan Ramazani, Richard Ellmann, and Robert O'Clair. *Vol 1: Modern Poetry*. New York: W. W. Norton & Co., 2003. 806–808.

Bakhtin, Mikhail. *The Bakhtin Reader: Selected Writings of Bakhtin, Medvedev and Voloshinov*. Ed. Pam Morris. London: Edward Arnold, 1994.

Crane, Stephen. "In a Desert." *The Oxford Book of American Poetry*. Ed. David Lehman. Oxford: Oxford UP, 2006. 203–204.

Coleridge, Samuel Taylor. "The Rime of the Ancient Mariner." *Lyrical Ballads*. William Wordsworth and Samuel Taylor Coleridge. Oxford: Oxford UP, 2013. 5–24.

Dickinson, Emily. *The Complete Poems of Emily Dickinson*. Boston: Little, Brown, and Company, 1924. Online publication in June 2000 by Bartleby. com. http://www.bartleby.com/113/4031.html

Finkelstein, Norman. *The Objects in Your Life*. Atlanta: House of Keys, 1977.

———. *The Ratio of Reason to Magic: New & Selected Poems*. Loveland, OH: Dos Madres Press, Inc., 2016.

Freud, Sigmund. *On Dreams*. New York: W. W. Norton & Co., 1980.

---

10. See W. H. Auden's "In Praise of Limestone" in the *Norton Anthology of Modern and American Poetry, Volume 1: Modern Poetry.*

Homer. *The Odyssey*. Trans. by Robert Fagles. Intro and notes by Bernard Knox. New York: Penguin, 1996.

Huk, Romana. Book Review of *On Mount Vision: Forms of the Sacred in Contemporary American Poetry*. *Religion & Literature*, 44.1 (Spring 2012): 225–231.

Irving, Washington. "Rip Van Winkle." *The Complete Tales of Washington Irving*. Ed. and intro. Charles Neider. New York: Da Capo Press, Inc., 1998. 1–16.

Scroggins, Mark. Book Review of *Not One of Them in Place: Modern Poetry and Jewish American Identity*. *Shofar: An Interdisciplinary Journal of Jewish Studies* 21.1 (Fall 2002): 126–128.

Yeats, William Butler. "The Fool by the Roadside." Online access at *Poem Hunter*. 1/3/17. https://www.poem

To Love Too Much: Norman Finkelstein and the Problem of Inscription

Burt Kimmelman

Norman Finkelstein is the inheritor of an aesthetics and ethics whose collective force, in American poetry and poetics, has been considerable, in part because of what he has written. Now, as I look back over that body of work, I feel that what I'd written about it fell short, having missed what best defines it, what a volume like *The Ratio of Reason to Magic* (a milestone in his splendid career),[1] in part retrospective, makes salient. In Finkelstein's poetry, residing at the heart of his experience, is a concern for *text*. It manifests thematically and stylistically, holding as one belief and praxis.

That his work uniquely attends to his life as a Jew—in his poems this means his life as a poet—has everything to do with how his world, through his poetics, comes to life. Finkelstein is a poet who has never taken his Judaism for granted, who has always lived and acted as a Jew, then as a Jew who is a poet. I wonder if I could, alternatively, say that he has lived and acted as a poet who is also someone whose Judaism underlies his life. Finkelstein's Jewish way of life, so to speak, can be a religious way of life, specifically a religious practice; there's an equally religious practice that's obvious to me in his writing, which involves his vocation of poet, containing a certain complexity having directly to do with the nature of Judaism. Even so, this complexity, which is grounded in text itself, is prominent in the work of some poets who are not Jews.

Among living Jewish American poets whose work informs Finkelstein's, three especially stand forth: Jerome Rothenberg and

---

1. Hereafter cited as *RRM*.

Michael Heller for many reasons, and Hank Lazer insofar as some of his poetry, in both outlook and style, I associate with Finkelstein's great trilogy *Track*. Other Jewish American poets, who are now gone, have also fed a collective experience constituting, for Finkelstein, a way of seeing. Yet some of the poets whose work has guided Finkelstein's monumental achievement have not been Jews. George Oppen and Armand Schwerner were Jews, while William Bronk, Robert Duncan and Jack Spicer were not. So, in my trying to explain Finkelstein now, especially as I better understand how central in his imagination and art Judaic thought has been, I realize that the poetry is not simply Jewish, either in terms of theme, let's say, or style. All the work, however, is textual.

His work emerges from this web of association to form an impression peculiar to it: the feeling that Finkelstein has been writing the same poem, a poem still not finished, since he first took pen to paper. The fact that this poem is essentially textual, moreover, imbues it with insight drawn from these other poets, gentiles and Jews. But the Judaic tradition is principally textual in nature, fundamentally and uniquely so. In any case, the poem is still to be finished, and this is decidedly Jewish in nature.

Do my contradictions have anything to do with what I'd say is the paradox of Finkelstein's unfinished poem, which tells me something about what Judaism was always meant to be, despite God's curse in choosing the Jews to be unique among all peoples? I ask this particular question, now, as I read Finkelstein's beautifully self-divining lyric "אמת" (the title poem from *Restless Messengers*, 1992); this Hebrew can be translated into English as "truth."

The poem's epigraph bespeaks my characterization of Finkelstein's poetic-life project. I note that its dedication is to William Bronk, someone whose poetry was always about, and embodied, a radical epistemology, and whose work was always mindful of its textual commission (Bronk was a most careful poet). The poem reads as follows.

תמא

You are not required to complete the work, but neither are you free to desist
from it.
—Rabbi Tarphon, *Pirkei Vot*

for William Bronk

Have I loved the Torah more than God,
sailing in an ark to the homeland of the text:
or have I been recalled by a handful of slogans,
      the leaking resonance of glamorous tropes
         reduced to empty shells?

      The primal vowel is caught in the throat:
aleph, the utterance which precedes the truth
in which is contained the formula of negation,
      mem and *tav*: to be found at last
         inscribed on any forehead.

      The clay collapses upon the creator,
         the letters lie in a heap:
or freed from the flesh, do they rise upward,
         seeking the limiting code?

Bound and unbound to the limits of the world:
      Covenant prior to all known covenants:
from a displaced source come restless messengers
         yearning for authority from absent kings. (*RRM* 32)

Earlier poems by Finkelstein hint at a developing sensibility and
what I might call, perhaps, an ideology, one that aligns Finkelstein with
a poet like Bronk. Indeed, notice this poem from Finkelstein's very early
collection, *The Objects in Your Life*, titled "The World":

Not a ring of light. The world has been translated.
The sky touches the earth at all points, and light
is at once perceived. The houses, the street corners,
glow with light. An inchoate expression of source,
for the earth/universal is changing.

From the pages of a book, I see how thought
disseminates into the world. And the world is filled
with the comings and goings of men and women.
And this is the dream of the world, this
marriage to itself, and not abandoned.

The bridegroom comes for the bride. (8)

Let's compare the above lines with a portion of one of Finkelstein's recent poems, "Meeting" (one of the "new" poems in *The Ratio of Reason to Magic*, which is part of a collection titled *From the Files of the Immanent Foundation*). This "new" poem falls back upon the same language, the same tropes, in some ways the same concerns—yet now in the service of another cause, that being Finkelstein's surreal and mythical "foundation" of being, which takes the guise of *immanence*. The "meeting," signaled in the poem's title, is made up of "sectarians" who are "gathered in [an] almond grove." There, it happens that the "Completists are willing to speak"; they're absolutists. "*All or Nothing-at-*All, declare their banners."

The poem tells us that "letters" of a "history," a "chronicle" someone is "trying to write," have a particular relationship; they "correspond to the original pattern on the scroll." Furthermore, the poem explains,

These letters constitute a correspondence
that would appear to have been completed
before the city was abandoned. These letters
were found in a box, but these, which complete the set,
fell from the sky [...]. (*RRM* 326)

This poem is spelling out a personal and intellectual, I dare say poetic, ideology Finkelstein has been in communion with throughout his career. The repetition of "letters" in itself is, in this way, telling. There's this curious situation, one fraught with mystical overtones generated by an allegory of abstraction. He has gravitated toward this ploy in his later years. Yet his attentions, the terms of his poetry, have in fact been consistent, indeed ever-dwelling, throughout his life as poet.

Surely what drives Finkelstein's intellectual search is epistemological, not unlike Bronk's. More keenly, I mean to say there has always been a sustained and methodical meditation on being itself, in his poems. There's never a stridency in them. What there is, on the other hand, as I look back in them as a body of work, is an existential urgency.

I refuse to believe that in his adult life, as I read through the poems now, Finkelstein ever anguished over whether he loved the Torah more than God. Of course he did. I don't believe Finkelstein is, in other words, a Jewish Thomas Merton. I love the story of the adolescent who's being tutored by a rabbi, which goes like this: Having pored over scripture together for some considerable time, they pause. From within the ensuing silence the student murmurs, "Rabbi, I don't believe in God." A further silence—then the rabbi replies, "Don't worry about it."

Is this rabbi the shrewd teacher who knows better than to enforce doctrine? Finkelstein manages to explore ideas with doubt and understated reverence, at times with awe such that, of necessity, it rises to the level of myth or perhaps mysticism, as something of a singularly beautiful quest.

Unlike in Rothenberg, even perhaps in Heller who is Finkelstein's unannounced interlocutor in many of the poems—note the presence of Gershom Scholem as well as Walter Benjamin in their respective published works (abundantly so in the personal correspondence with one another)—the quest seems paramount. The quest is not for existential meaning but rather existential vibrancy, which is only possible when the inquiry is founded in the love of reading and writing, and when it need not seek a conclusion or "meaning"—in other words, as Mark Scroggins puts it an essay on *Track*, when it involves "endlessly multiplying midrashim." About Finkelstein, Claudia Keelan eloquently observes that "[n]o contemporary figure's life project more avidly scours the borders between heaven and earth, doctrine and faith, the metaphysical inside the physical spaces of a Word" (97).

The *Track* trilogy (2002, 2012) comes along in mid-career for Finkestein. It's when, I think, his poetics arrives at its maturity. He's not so much, any longer, searching as a poet—I don't mean any longer as a thinker. Instead, he's busy filling out an achieved métier. "The Telling"—a poem from Finkelstein's *Passing Over* (2007)—concludes with these lines: Words / remain / after all else is consumed" (RRM 94). For Finkelstein, "the passage of time / grows perceptible / here among the passages / of notes or text," as he writes in *Columns*, the second volume of the *Track* trilogy (RRM 159). In that book, too, we might find him "Wandering in the passage / between the words and the things" (RRM 161). The work, after the trilogy, will not leave off such a meditation. Instead, it expands it within a greater range, better to say within a greater magnitude of poetic power, of artistic possibility.

Here is a moving lapse into incantation, the penultimate section of Finkelstein's "Desert" (from Scribe, 2009):

Neither upon the sky nor upon the ground

Neither in the desert nor at the mountain

Neither in the heights nor in the depths

Neither present nor absent

Neither known nor unknown

Neither strange nor familiar

Neither whole nor in fragments

Neither revealed nor hidden

Neither sacred nor profane

Neither spoken nor silent. (*RRM 229*)

After the publication of *Scribe,* I wrote about the preceding trilogy as a work that didn't merely symbolize but also linked a strain in American poetry I saw as running from Oppen, through Schwerner, then Heller to Finkelstein, uniting a lineage ("*Tracking* the Word," 2009). I realized what the *Track* trilogy had accomplished in some literary-critical way—which was to make this lineage vivid, thus calling attention to its significance within the larger procession of American poetry, or at least the American avant-garde poetry. It was only with the materialization of the trilogy that something shared by the four poets, of descending ages, was made especially plain. This had much to do with Judaism.

I concluded that "text is the Jew's reality, and it is a source of his exile as well" (51). Exile is the consequence, paradoxically perhaps, of the bestowal of the Torah. Hence the condition of Judaism, whatever apart it may be intellectually, is that of the Jewish Diaspora. At the heart of the Diaspora lies, to borrow from Beth Sharon Ash,

> the paradoxical situation of the exegete's submission to the oldest revelation at Sinai and yet freedom for new interpretation of the Divine Word through the strange midrashic conversation. This intertextual dialogue, conducted for thousands of years by multiple voices who understand one another as contemporaries, must also continually reformulate meanings relevant to the adjudication of current problems in Jewish life. Since the text is central to this historical process, the boundaries between the Word and its interpretation are more fluid, more open to narrative retelling than we usually imagine for scripture. (68)

Ash may wish to confine herself to Jewish *scripture,* but I want to expand the scope of midrash meant to "continually reformulate meanings relevant to the adjudication of current problems" [above]). I return now to Finkelstein's poem "תמה," which I can read as an early, albeit pivotal, work in his *oeuvre.* The poem dramatizes, for its author and for its readers too, and promises what his poetry became in its full efflorescence. The poem is nearly a map of his journey.

In this context, I think especially of what came to be known in the West as *the exegetical tradition,* that which defined Christianity, in my view. I'm not making a trivial observation here—in other words, if we consider the history of the Jewish Diaspora up to and including the present (whatever the State of Israel has been or will become). This Diaspora, the "primal vowel," poetry, and the "truth," all form a key image in Finkelstein's ideology.

The Hebrew word for "Truth" is made up of *aleph, mem,* and *tav*; these three characters (as worded above in the second stanza of Finkelstein's poem "תמא" or "Truth") contain this word's inner "negation" that is "to be found at last / inscribed on any forehead." This ideology becomes subsumed in his poetics. It's the artistry of a poetry that rightfully glorifies the dispensation of language, more to the point of inscription, which in turn makes human self-realization within the greater community possible. Finkelstein understands—beyond any doctrinaire rendering—what the force of that inscription "on any forehead" is.

That the *tefillin* (in the Hebrew)—part of which holds *scripture* in a leather box, inscription, applied to the supplicant's forehead in prayer—is made of leather is of deep significance. This image and fact deeply roots Finkelstein's poetry. According to a comment in the Torah, the leather is required. The *tefillin* must be worn "in order that the Torah of Hashem [God] shall be in your mouth" (Shemot 13:9 [cf. Daily Halacha]).

In the later Augustine's *Confessions* there's a passage whose metaphorical power, I have come to think, is directly Judaic in origin. It's all too easy to underestimate, in the early Christian era as well as the ensuing Middle Ages, how central *text* was to understanding life, even material existence. Language—indeed, over time, inscription— was at the heart of it all. John writes, "In the beginning was the Word." The Torah on the forehead is "in" the observant Jew's "mouth" through prayer, speech, language, written language.

This Judaic dispensation ultimately says something essential about the Jewish Diaspora, and thereby about the condition of the believer. Finkelstein is the poet who "[loves] the Torah more than God." Although we see a similar struggle in the *Confessions,* on the part of Augustine on his way to spiritual enlightenment, I wonder now if this "fault," on the part of the Finkelstein persona, is unique to the practicing Jew, while Augustine the writer also makes use of it.

What Christianity did was to reverse this hierarchy. With the *tefillin,* mind and body and word are one. Being is textual. In the *Confessions* (XIII.15), as he alludes to a biblical passage, Augustine articulates his sense of the eternal as a heavenly text—specifically (echoing Apocalypse 6:14), he pictures that text as a furled scroll. In contrast, he then imagines the created world as unfurled, "spread out like a canopy of skins" (as in vellum). In describing the manifest world, creation, he exploits a biblical inter-association of skin, clothing, scroll, text and language.

Augustine conceived of the mortal world, the medievalist scholar Eugene Vance writes, as a "scroll of the firmament, a layer of 'skin'" (i.e., parchment as well as garment) on which "the primal dictation of creation is dispensed as a written text, as Scripture" (8). The metaphor of inscription, with an already long history, continued into the later Middle Ages. Hugh of St. Victor described the world as a book written by the hand of God, while St. Bonaventure's notion of the Book of Nature emphasized not the image of the book itself but, instead, the act of reading that joins the reader to it.

Finkelstein's poetry depicts this reader, the young man who loves the Torah too much, himself. Finally, Finkelstein is a secular poet. Yet he's a devout Jew insofar as he has experienced the textual nature of poetry and turned his own poetry toward making that nature manifest. To his credit, his poems, and he himself, have been "Bound and unbound to the limits of the world" (above)—bound like the supplicant is bound, wearing the *tefillin* on hand, arm and head.

"תמה" is a crucial poem in the Finkelstein *oeuvre* not because, in later poems, he would not surpass its graceful and moving artistry, but, instead, because it was prophetic in naming the struggle the young poet would engage in his writing thereafter. A linguistic skepticism, which he's located at the heart of the Judaic intellectual and religious tradition, resonates in some lines by Oppen—an untaught Jew—and I note the difference in tone between Finkelstein's "תמא" and Oppen's "A Language of New York" (1965), especially in these lines: "Possible / To use / Words provided one treat them / As enemies."

Oppen's passage was not so prophetic, after all, I can now say in hindsight. Finkelstein, along with Heller especially, learned the lesson Oppen had to teach, nonetheless. What comes through in their work, in the last analysis, is the love of inscription. There's perhaps merely a difference in emphasis. In any case, for Finkelstein, through that love, the world and the self are realized.

Works Cited

Saint Augustine. *Confessions*. Ed. and Tr. R. S. Pine-Coffin. London: Penguin, 1961.

Augustinus, Aurelius. *Confessiones*. Knöll's editio minor, 1898. Transcription J. J. O'Donnell, Oxford, UK: Oxford UP, 1992. Online.

Vance, Eugene. "Augustine's *Confessions* and the Grammar of Selfhood." *Genre* 6 (1973): 1–28.

Ash, Beth Sharon. "Jewish Hermeneutics and Contemporary Theories of Textuality: Hartman, Bloom, and Derrida." *Modern Philology* 85.1 (August 1987): 65–80.

Finkelstein, Norman. *The Objects In Your Life*. Atlanta: House of Keys, 1977.

———. *Passing Over*. East Rockaway, NY: Marsh Hawk Press, 2007.

———. *Restless Messengers*. Athens, GA: University of Georgia Press, 1992.

———. *The Ratio of Reason to Magic: New & Selected Poems*. Loveland, OH: Dos Madres Press, 2016.

———. *Scribe*. Loveland, OH: Dos Madres Press, 2009.

———. *Track* [3 vols.: *Forest*, *Columns*, and *Powers*]. Bristol, UK: Shearsman Books, 2012.

Keelan, Claudia. "The Possible Sacred: On Track to the Sublime in Norman Finkelstein's Poetry." *Talisman: A Journal of Contemporary Poetry and Poetics* (Fall 2006).

Kimmelman, Burt. "The Presence and Absence of the Text: Norman Finkelstein's Recent and Early Poetry" [Review Essay Retrospective of *Restless Messengers, Passing Over,* and *Track* (*Track, Powers,* and *Columns*) by Norman Finkelstein], *Galatea Resurrects* 8 (30 November 2007). Online.

———. "*Tracking* the Word: Judaism's Exile and the Writerly Poetics of George Oppen, Armand Schwerner, Michael Heller, and Norman Finkelstein." *Shofar: An Interdisciplinary Journal of Jewish Studies* 27.3 (Spring 2009): 30-51.

Daily Halacha Entry: "The Leather Used for the Parchment Inside the Tefillin and the Tefillin Boxes." Daily Halacha. Online.

Scroggins, Mark. "Review of Norman Finkelstein, *Track.*" *Jacket* 11 (April 2000). Online.

A Petite Book, A Little Exile

Tyrone Williams

A book event: Shortly after the 1999 publication of the first volume of *Track*, I wrote the following, long-ish, introduction to a reading Norman Finkelstein was about to give:

> Norman Finkelstein is the author of three books of literary criticism—*The Utopian Moment In Contemporary American Poetry*, *The Ritual of New Creation* and, forthcoming, *Not One Of Them In Place*—as well as two books of poetry, *Restless Messengers* and the just-published *Track*. Recent essays of his appear in *Contemporary Literature*, *Religion & Literature*, and *The Objectivist Nexus*.

> If one were to map the trajectory of Norman's critical and creative writings over the past decade, one could not help but notice that his essays, poems, articles and books enact the condition of the late 20th century ethnic writer awashed in Americana. His is the writing of the visitor who has only his permanent visa to legitimize his stay, one which he bears in his blood, wears on his body, in his surname, a permanent stamp of approval that can always—as history teaches us—be revoked.

> The experience of permanent exile, permanent deferment of meaningfulness, conditions all his writings, and to that extent, and perhaps more, they call into question the very distinction between "criticism" and "creativity." By now, of course, the distinction as well as its deconstruction is old hat, and were these writings unaware of their belated entry into the confused and confusing arena of "modernism" and "postmodernism," they would simply fall into either camp. But like that of several other contemporary American writers—and artists in general—Norman's writings teeter precariously on the fine,

often blurred, line between modernism and postmodernism, between criticism or poetry and hypercritical poetry and poetic criticism. This fence-walking, this tightrope balancing act, can often appear, perhaps can only appear, as simply another form of aestheticism, as yet another overwrought, over-acculturated, "ethnic" sensibility, all too anxious to demonstrate it "belongs" to a culture in which it remains suspect. Or it can always betray the whiff of the incorrigible stranger, the airs it puts on notwithstanding. In short, Norman's writings, as an American poet and critic, as a Jewish American poet and critic, can always be read as an historically determined willful obscurity, not unlike, not surprisingly, the willful balkanization of those who simply will not learn how to speak "proper" English, those who stubbornly insist on their slang, dialects, ebonics, Spanglish, what have you.

Need I add that these readings, which are in fact the predominant readings of "our" culture, are profound misreadings? Profound because they betray the xenophobia that hides behind every form of right-minded thinking, profound because the excavation of the sedimentation of Christian history, so often conflated with Western history, demands a poetics that calls into question every commonplace articulated in what we so easily call "our language." And misreadings because they insist on "translating" this language he still troubles to speak, still worries to writing, into "English," into "reading." For me, Norman's poetry and criticism, at their richest, at their most disturbing, dance and lurch toward the consolations of "pen-membering," an awkward wave of the hand that bids farewell to the body and hello to the book.

Another book event: At a fall 2016 poetry reading in Cincinnati celebrating the publication of his *Selected and New Poems*, Norman Finkelstein confided to a small but attentive audience that he was "bookish," that his poems derive largely from the books he reads. Finkelstein was the third or fourth reader that evening; he followed several spoken-word, performance-oriented, poets whose recitations found a ready audience at a downtown bar whose reading series favors performance-oriented poets and poetry. So I took his admission as a bit defensive, as a warning that he wouldn't be "performing" his poetry if performing meant listener-friendly declamations of current political and social issues. It was hardly the place or time to do so, and so he didn't remind his audience, and perhaps himself, that between rap- or Beat-inflected poems and what we call the world is language, textuality, spoken and written, without which the world exists as only an inscrutable kaleidoscope of colors and sounds if one is born with sight and hearing. He didn't remind them, or himself, that there is nothing outside those spoken and written words, the contexts in which they are framed. Nevertheless, anyone who has read Finkelstein and listened to or read spoken word poetry knows that there are differences between what he does and what they do. And those differences are not, as I just suggested, simply textual but rather contextual and intertextual, his insistence on braiding together strands from many books. In that sense, we might imagine Finkelstein as always writing, always cloaked in, a many-braided book. And we need not look to recent history, much less the current miasma engulfing the cultural landscape, to recall the long history of suspicion directed at the book and book readers. Any philosopher, historian, theologian, or literary scholar knows these histories. From the general perspective of societies indigenous and colonial, ancient and modern, there has always been something cultish about book readers, to say nothing of the books themselves, books as allegedly innocuous as romances and mysteries, and books, more darkly, associated with religious and academic coteries and disciplines. And I will assume I do not need to rehearse here, in this academic space called a book, the insidious associations between anti-books (and, more generally, anti-intellectualism) and antisemitism. So when Finkelstein proudly, and perhaps defensively, proclaims his allegiance to books, he is not simply standing up for a long intellectual tradition. He is also, however implicitly, standing up for the right to remain a Jewish-American reader and writer free to raid Judaic and Gentile cultural storehouses for aesthetic profit.[1] Put this way, the critical and creative endeavors of Finkelstein (and others) can always be read as suspicious, and thus dangerous, moments in a long history of suspicion

---

1. Finkelstein explicitly makes this point in the short essay "Total Midrash."

directed at interpretation from within and without Jewish cultures and diasporas, especially when the interpretation of interpretation can easily, deliberately, be interpreted as cause and effect of usury, to say nothing of the usury of usury.[2]

Why invoke usury as one effect of the well-known Derridean "interpretation of interpretation"? Insofar as interpretation is another formulation of Derrida's insistence that there is nothing outside the text, the interpretation of interpretation remains within this formulation but points to specific cultural, social and, above all, economic textualities.[3] Zooming out from Finkelstein's poetry, we can see that those others I parenthetically cited above are also implicated in what I am calling the usury of usury, compounding the interest on interest. This is not simply another way of citing an exoticism whose principal is the accumulation of a certain kind of primitivism, those readymade stereotypes always at hand. It is also a gift, an amassed principal, a form of economic privilege, and a mode of primitive accumulation. It is a gift in precisely the sense that Derrida gives the term, another mode of the pharmakon.[4] Norman Finkelstein is a part of the current generation of American poets for whom individual identity is stereotyped as a shorthand for group identity, an ethnos and purportedly non-ethnos brought together and kept apart from "other" Americans, that is, an anthropological identity hyphenated according to the categories of the Census of Bureau's ethnic and racial categories. He is, in effect, an "ethnic" American poet. This structure makes no sense outside the standard it implicitly privileges: the non-ethnic American, aka, the "white" American. To the extent he himself writes and criticizes according to this model Finkelstein draws interest on the interest in Jewish American writing. We who are not Jewish but who

2. In this sense Finkelstein's flirtation with Gnosticism, primarily by way of Robert Duncan, can be understood as another mode of aestheticism, that is, as anti-Gnostic. As Patrick Pritchett puts it in an article on Michael Palmer, the burnt book must be thought, within a certain tradition, as a necessary condition for the venerated book.
3. For a recent summary of Derrida's position see John W P Phillips' "A Guide to Jacques Derrida's "Structure, Sign and Play in the Discourse of the Human Sciences" at https://courses.nus.edu.sg/course/elljwp/structuresign.htm.
4. See "Plato's Pharmacy" in Derrida's *Dissemination*.

are nonetheless drawn to this poetry because of its supposedly "Jewish" elements draw interest on his interest in the interest in Jewish American poetry. That this formulation is analogous to the financialization of capital is hardly coincidental since the question in general of "interest" is ineluctably economic.[5] There are actual economic effects at play, not the least of which is the publication history of Finkelstein's books of poetry and criticism. Zooming out even farther to see the larger landscape of the poetry business, provided by magazines like *Poets & Writers*, for example, we see that ethnic poetry is, once again, all the rage. African American poets—or rather, a certain kind of African American poet— had it good in the 1920s and then again in the 1960s. And despite the current focus on poets from the African and Asian continents, African American poets have been able to ride the coat-tails of the vogue for the trans (-national, -sexual, etc.) fetish. What this means, however, for Jewish American poets of Finkelstein's generation is that their fifteen minutes of attention from the po'biz (and this includes "mainstream" as well as "alternative" institutions) may be drawing to a close.

Nonetheless, these social, cultural, and economic conditions under which Finkelstein writes are not the only reasons for the apparent eclipse—or perhaps temporary waning—of a general interest in Jewish American poetry. The exceptionalism of Jewish American poetry has depended, in part, on its fetishization of the book, and Finkelstein has followed, if not always faithfully, in turning over and over this fetish. Reading through the *New & Selected* one cannot help but notice the various ways the book, to say nothing of bookishness, insinuates itself into the very fabric of Finkelstein's poetry and poetics. But while the book remains the standard of legitimacy within both literary and non- or para-literary institutions even as it morphs into the e-book, which retains all the ideological features and thus induces all the aesthetic and para-aesthetic presumptions of the cloth and paper book, the book, whatever its material or virtual form, has lost some of its hegemonic potency as textuality in general overruns the borders that enable genre, gender and

---

5. In short, the commodification of Jewish American poetry allows it to function within Marx's famous schema M-C-M, its surplus value reducible to "interest" in every sense of the word.

gentility.[6] It goes without saying that these alterations in the cultural, social, political and economic landscapes cannot be simply subsumed under the categories of either "progress" or "regress." Yet, within Jewish American literary traditions, these changes do not augur well for a certain way of reading and interpreting generations of Jewish American poets leading up to and including Finkelstein's. For if, within this tradition, every book is only a diminutive derivative of the Book, itself a shard or fragment from a destroyed Temple, then Finkelstein's books, like those of all Jewish American poets of his generation, are even smaller, even more diminished, even, we might say, more *petite* than the previous generation's books.[7] The ambiguous, feminine connotations of this French term are pertinent insofar as the book, whatever its volume, is a symptom of dispersal and exile; the book is thus a vessel, even a Trojan Horse, for "foreign" languages, which is to say, for contamination and impurity. Moreover, as Maeera Shreiber has shown, exile and dispersal are, within a certain Jewish tradition, linked to women.[8] Shreiber traces this lineage back to Rachael in the Torah. She is, perhaps, the first "wailing woman," and though Shreiber does not draw out the implications of her analysis per the *general* problem of Jewish American poetry (she is interested in rehabilitating certain Jewish American women poets), we can see how, within an allegedly "non-ethnic" American context, the Jewish American

---

6. Thus the institutions upheld by their respective frameworks, and this includes, per gentility, cultural democracy, free speech and sexual propriety, are under siege by various modes of populism (e.g., call-out culture, fake news, and leftist censorship). No political, economic, social or cultural value remains sacrosanct.

7. And so we find ourselves in a position where the Bloomian labyrinths of psychic drives are the internalized remain(der)s of diaspora after diaspora, where, as we will see, Maeera Shreiber's insights re "sowing" dovetail with Harold Bloom's "strong poets." As Finkelstein puts it in "A Tomb for Northrup Frye," "—I, a Jew for whom all is interminable." (57)

8. In "The End of Exile: Jewish Identity and Its Diasporic Poetics," Shreiber praises Alain Finkielkraut's *The Imaginary Jew*, noting its attempt to decouple diaspora from Jewish women: "In diagnosing Diaspora as a condition of lack, embodied in the ever-mournful mother, Finkielkraut identifies a crucial gendered opposition long implicit in the dominant constructions of Jewish identity—constructions that set an idealized vision of home as whole against a view of exile-as-diaspora as perpetually broken, the feminine body figuring prominently in both cases." (277)

male poet is himself another incarnation of the wailing woman, that is, a man who, having lost his land, having not returned to his land, can only sing of his failures—like a woman. However, as Shreiber points out, diaspora and exile are not the same experiences. There can be, she argues, potency, and thus rejuvenation, in refusing the comforts of familiarity, family and home.[9]

For Finkelstein, refusal goes only so far, just a little farther. His no—which is not, for example, Blake's Nobodaddy—takes him to the wilderness of Gnosticism which, in a strictly nonethnic American context, means little despite the country's paid advertisements of "In God We Trust." But within a specific Jewish American tradition, this move takes Finkelstein far, if not too far, into the forest of transmogrifications. Let's call this "state" a little exile.

And so we return to, zoom back in on, Finkelstein's poetry as collected in the New & Selected. What might we imagine going through the head of a largely disinterested reader of Finkelstein's writings, which is to say, what about the nonpartisan reader of what Finkelstein has been reading, however transmogrified into "poetry" or "criticism"? If we imagine that such an agnostic reader exists, how might she interpret this transmogrification? Yes, transmogrification, for Finkelstein often takes glee in conjoining, by bending or twisting—braiding, if you will—Judaic and Gentile texts, sacred and secular writings, into what some, Jewish and not, might regard as monstrosities. At the same time, or specifically, much earlier in his career, Finkelstein seemed, and still seems, less prone to devilish nose-thumbing than respectful mimicry. But that kind of homage often wound up, still winds up, leading to revelations darker than the source-texts might otherwise imply. For example, in "A Poem for the Great Heresy," God's "return" to one of his creations is both belated and impossible (how can that which is eternal return?). God's divine curiosity or vigilance is blocked by human interpretation of God's interpretation (collected in the Book) of humanity, and inasmuch as both interpretations appear interminable until the fullness of time, we remain, are forced to remain, on our own, self-sufficient:

---

9. Sheiber notes that the etymological denotations of diaspora include not only "to scatter" but also "to sow."

> God is a face pressed
> against the window panes
> of attics, basements, abandoned houses,
> where in closets beneath staircases
> still may be found
> the traces of a secondary, hibernal creation (35)

These lines underscore Finkelstein's belief, articulated here and elsewhere, that reading and writing "complete" the narrative of creation by circling back, tracing the arc of mythic temporality, a process which disarticulates creation from origin by doubling down on the former, a not so unusual move associated with the apotheosis of "genius" in the English Romantics. Because our hypothetical reader is agnostic, this theme, we imagine, may pass over her head. At this point, if not before, she may put the book down and move on to what she will understand as more important things of this world. On the other hand, can either a "believer" or a "nonbeliever" accept at face value these lines or relish in their mimicry of satanic verses? Or is it the case that only a gnostic sensibility can, as we say, appreciate these lines, which is to say, monetize them beyond mere aesthetics? In brief, can only a certain kind of bookish reader "get" this type of bookish poet? With the *New & Selected* in hand as Exhibit A, are we justified in situating this poem as "characteristically" bookish and therefore one explanation, if not justification, for the apparently little exile of the "early" Finkelstein?

Is, that is, the mischievous Finkelstein a more recent "development"? And does this newfangled impishness stand in for a stereotype, the "Jewish" Finkelstein? Let's say our agnostic reader has just lifted her head from the page after reading, "You've been listening to Radio Free Hell." (270) What does it mean that the second person invoked here, singular or plural, is simultaneously a reader and a listener, a commonplace hybrid captured in the trite expression "it says" when the "it" is a written text? What does it mean for a Jewish American poet to invoke "hell" as an occulted radio station, sending its signals up, through, into, indeed, as, books? Moreover, the syntax of this line suggests that "Hell' can broadcast itself without the aid of material media, a hell free of the radio. Insofar as this line, however read, conjures the specter of Spicer, it seems to be one of those places in the *New & Selected* where the "ratio" between magic (speaking) and reason (reading) is explicitly invoked, not just as a philosophical or literary calibration but, specifically, as a mathematical definition of the book. True, "The book/ is the history of the book," (299) but is it the case that the book is subversive per se, that is, subversive not because of its "contents" but because it is simply—and not so simply—a book, a curio irreducible to any discipline or practice, occult or empirical? A book that is a book no matter what language inhabits it? And obviously a book no matter its shape or form, no matter its paper or electronic materiality. One could argue that suspicions regarding books concern, for the most part, not the book per se but rather the dangers of unsupervised reading, which is why, as one example, early nineteenth-century college students, like the pre-Vulgate Catholic laity, were not permitted to read books without the supervision of their teachers. Here would be examples of readings, of textualities that, per Derrida, exceed the limits imposed by the book, a general, unrestricted, economy of interpretation that, as noted above, threatens the integrity of every borderline. This kind of reading, interpretation, and usury, can take one far afield, which is why these kinds of transgressions have often been subjected to the most sanguine and the most ruthless punishments. For every unauthorized interpretation or reading implicitly names another interpretation or reading "error." We should never forget the "lesson" imparted by the first book of *The Faerie Queen*. Sir Knight strangles the she-beast, a kind of Medusa figure, who, in her death throes, throws up,

> A flood of Poison horrible and black,
> Full of great Lumps of Flesh and Gobbets raw,
> Which stunk so vildly, that it forc'd him slack
> His grasping hold, and from her turn him back:
> Her Vomit full of Books and Papers....

Even if we read *The Faerie Queen* as evidence of little more than another kind of bookish poet trying to, if you'll pardon the precolonial anachronism, curry favor with the church by inveighing against books, the fact is the book itself, and Spenser's is no exception, is a dangerous potion, if not poison, a concoction of ingredients from other magical potions, poisons, and concoctions. These vile ingredients are ideas and images from other books, mere notions, innocuous metaphors, that one imbibes simply by reading, and then, worst, infecting others simply by writing: "and the books and papers reach back toward that Infinity / from which the books and papers are said to come" (59). Just as the premodern linguists' presumption that the Hebraic "residues" quickening modern languages in direct proportion to each language's age implies that linguistic, and thus sacred, continuity was but a fraying rope tied to the Temple, so too the proliferation of "books and papers" implicates the Midrashic tradition as another symptom of nonlethal debilitation, a petite sign of impotence and, per Bloom, Shreiber, Finkelstein and the entire Gnostic tradition, potency.[10]

Given writing and thus books as various strains of influenza, oral transmission would seem to be the best way to pass on traditions more or less purified of other traditions, sacred or secular but, fortunately and unfortunately, human memory is fallible, susceptible to suggestion, a flaw that Plato, infamously, blames, in part, on writing, a tradition whose very existence is not only a threat to orality but a portent of the book that is no longer a "score" for oral performativity but is, instead, a self-sufficient conglomerate and archive of oral sophistry. This "other" tradition, a tradition of ceaseless inscription as negativity incarnate, is invoked in the poem "Instructions for the King": "None of this may be written down, for it may be forgotten, / and it is not to be forgotten" (256). This poem is placed fairly deep into the *New & Selected*, and though similar injunctions have already been invoked throughout the book, they contradict concomitant *dis*junctions throughout the collection, that memory, however idealized by Plato and others, is also

---

10. For the premodern—that is, pre-Saussure et al—linguists, the older a language the more inspirited it is simply because it is "closer" to the original Aramaic in which Jesus spoke. Having no contact with this urlanguage, the linguists elected Hebrew as the next-best standard against which all other languages are found, to varying degrees, wanting. In this respect, Finkelstein, like other neo-Gnostics, tends to bypass or demote the insights of modern linguistics in favor of linguistics contemporary with the Romantics.

subject to corruption and erosion, baleful influences and degradation, before or outside the reign of writing. In short, Finkelstein plays the outsider that has already been ascribed to, written on, his body, itself a Jewish book (a white body, we are told, is not a book, has no history predating itself except when invoked as an emblem of a "tradition" or a "supremacy" irreducible to any ethnos). Finkelstein, surname of a non-white body and book, plays with the metaphysics and historicity attending memory's failure—moral failing or natural process— by insisting (the point is made in several poems), per Bloom and Barthes, that forgetting is a psycho-dramatic necessity, that forgetting clears psychic space for writing and reading. What this means is that translation, for example, is akin to writing; both erase as they preserve: "*Sign for 'folded' tent / translated as 'journey' // Sign for 'sea,' 'tablet' and 'wall' / translated as 'temple.'*" (182) Voice, like Benjamin's "original" language, is lost to the past, and retained for a future on the condition that it undergo transmogrification into writing. Needless to add, the above also describes the process of cultural assimilation, a one-way direction, says a white tradition, that Finkelstein must accept and must reject....

But loss of what we imagine as presence is not solely an effect of spatial or temporal distance. The present cannot guarantee anything since the moment we read and write what is read and what is written are already being forgotten. For who, indeed, can speak with vomit in one's mouth? Answer: everyone who speaks. For we only speak, we only write, with mouths teeming with vomit already transmogrified into "food / For future years," our *now* sliding irrevocably as nourishment or empty calories into future mouths. Undigested food, vomit, is projected forth in Borges' "Funes the Memorious." As you may recall, Ireno Funes is a 19-year-old man who suffers a crippling fall from a horse and, as a result, is "given" perfect perception and memory. Unable to sleep because he cannot forget, a parrot who can recite but never "speak," Funes eventually dies from the effects of his fall, congestion of the lungs. Yet his mind, if not his brain, was already dead, suffocated by his perfect memory. And yet, perfect memory, which is to say, perfect reading, a reading absent interpretation, is precisely what is demanded by certain political, theological, cultural and literary traditions. To misread, to misinterpret through interpretation, is forbidden, is, perhaps, merely a venial sin, but to willfully blend or braid a plethora of misinterpretations and misreadings, is a mortal sin, one that might explain why the poetry and criticism of Norman Finkelstein remains, however prominent, at the margins of contemporary American letters. In this little exile he remains stubbornly bookish; for too many book publishers and book readers, he's read, and he keeps reading, the wrong books, but wrong only, perhaps, now:

> **6.**
> So that in the future
> as in the past
>
> So that in the future
> not as in the past…

Works Cited

Derrida, Jacques. "Plato's Pharmacy." *Dissemination*. Trans. Barbara Johnson. Chicago: The University of Chicago Press, 1981, 63–171.

Finkelstein, Norman. *The Ratio Of Reason To Magic: New & Selected Poems*. Loveland, Ohio: Dos Madres Press, 2016.

———. "Total Midrash," *Religion & Literature*, 156–163.

Phillips, John W. P. "A Guide to Jacques Derrida's 'Structure, Sign and Play in the Discourse of the Human Sciences.'" https://courses.nus.edu.sg/course/elljwp/structuresign.htm

Pritchett, Patrick. "How To Write Poetry After Auschwitz: The Burnt Book of Michael Palmer." *Journal of Modern Literature*, 37:3, 127–145.

Shreiber, Maeera. "The End of Exile: Jewish Identity and Its Diasporic Poetics" *PMLA*, 113: 2 (March 1998), 273–287.

Code-Switching Across the Abyss: Norman Finkelstein's Fantastika

Mark Scroggins

With the publication of the three volumes of the serial poem *Track* around the turn of the millennium, Norman Finkelstein emerged as a major American poet, a figure to be discussed in company with such important writers of an earlier generation as Michael Palmer, Susan Howe, Ed Roberson, and Lyn Hejinian. But a decade and a half later, as Finkelstein has capped one period of his achievement with the selected poems *The Ratio of Reason to Magic,* and as he continues to break new ground with each successive book, his readers continue to be confronted with a question: what are we to do with Finkelstein's poetry? Yes, of course we read it, and celebrate it, and perhaps even analyze it. But for some of us—those with buttoned-down minds, with obsessively arranged and sorted bookcases: the anoraks, in short—the question arises, where do we *put* it? What do we call it?

To echo a much-loved phrase from Walter Benjamin, for the past fourteen months I have been unpacking my library (486). As I've opened each carton, the books that emerge get sorted—by language, by national origin, by genre—alphabetized by author's last name, arranged by publication date, and then shelved with their fellows: standard editions, art books, Victoriana, and major collections (Pound, Eliot, Joyce, Wyndham Lewis, Ruskin, the Objectivists) in the library; poetry criticism in the second floor hall; history and historiography in the basement; North American poetry in my study; and so forth.

Decanting one's books after a long spell is always an eye-opening experience. (Have I read this or not? what was I thinking when I

43

bought *that?*) But the endless process of taking volumes out of boxes, glancing at their spines, sometimes leafing through them and blushing at my own annotations, then sorting them into piles for their eventual shelving, has made me think about our principles of arranging books, about our principles of sorting literature in general, about the histories of mode, genres, and other pigeon-holes into which we shuffle linguisitic artefacts.[1] I've separated my books on British history from my books on American and European history; my mystery and detective novels (not an overwhelming number) are shelved in a different spot from my science fiction and fantasy books (a rather large collection), and each are in different places from more "realist" fiction. But Finkelstein's poetry books, from *The Objects in Your Life* (1977) to *The Ratio of Reason to Magic: New and Selected Poems* (2016), are there behind my desk in "poetry," nestled among the very disparate works of Annie Finch (Wiccan formalist), Norman Fischer (Zen experimentalist), Lisa Fishman (urban obliquitist), and Robert Fitterman (hard-nosed conceptualist).

I can't say I'm terribly satisfied with that spot. Indeed, there're times when I want to take Finkelstein's books and shelve them downstairs between Steven Erikson's *Gardens of the Moon* ("grimdark," cynical post-Tolkien fantasy) and William Gibson's *Neuromancer* (cyberpunk science fiction). In other words, one answer to that question about Finkelstein's poetry ("What do we call it?") is that we could call it *Fantastika*. I owe that word to one of my two or three favorite contemporary critics, the Canadian science fiction and fantasy scholar John Clute, whose knowledge of his chosen field is breathtakingly broad and detailed. Clute adopted the word "Fantastika" from various slavic roots to designate the "armamentarium of the fantastic in literature as a whole, encompassing science fiction, fantasy, fantastic horror and their various subgenres..." ("Fantastika"). It's a wonderfully broad umbrella term; it can at once shelter Joseph Sheridan Le Fanu's uncanny ghost stories, William Morris's dream-like romances, H. P. Lovecraft's scientifically justified tales of extraterrestrial eldritch horror, Ursula K. Le Guin's lovingly imagined Earthsea, Hal Clement's "hard" science fiction, and

---

1. Classic studies include Chartier and Fowler.

the unsettling, fractured realities of Philip K. Dick. Fantastika folds in all manner of fictions that violate the consensus-based experience we call "reality," and to that end the word is purposefully torqued, shifted from the more familiar "fantasy."

While all of the genres encompassed by "fantastika" intentionally violate the strictures of realism—they present worlds, and states of affairs within the world, that simply go against what we know to be "reality"—they do so in rather different manners (and historically to rather different ends) Samuel R. Delany, who has written ground-breaking work in both science fiction and fantasy, sums it up best to my mind as a difference in the "subjunctivities" of the genres: reportage—historical writing or journalism, for instance—takes place at the subjunctive level of "*this happened*"; naturalistic fiction's subjunctivity "is defined by: *could have happened*," fantasy's is "*could not have happened*," and science fiction's is "*have not happened*" (31–32, italics in original).

But our generic distinctions are by no means innocent of the marketplace, and while there is a clear kinship among the branches of fantastika—readers of Ursula K. Le Guin are more likely to be enthusiastic about Frank Herbert than about Joyce Carol Oates—there are also distinctions among them, enforced both by fannish (and academic) argument and by marketing and promotional strategies. If Barnes and Noble chooses to put Robert Heinlein ("science fiction") and J. R. R. Tolkien ("fantasy") in the same section, you can nonetheless be assured that their readers and their publishers are well aware of the distinction between the two realms. All of which is to say that part of the usefulness of Clute's "fantastika" is precisely its *difference* from "fantasy." "Fantasy," after all, has since roughly the 1970s come to designate among other things a commercially-defined genre.[2]

It has not always been so. In earlier moments, "fantasy" named not a genre but a mode of the imagination, a stepping beyond the boundaries of observable experience. Of course, it would be possible I think to

2. For a detailed discussion of the emergence of fantasy as a contemporary genre, see Williamson, *The Evolution of Modern Fantasy*; for a trenchant (if partisan and perhaps dated) account of the ontological and ethical differences between science fiction and fantasy, see Jameson, "The Great Schism" (57–71).

argue that "fantasy" and the "imagination" are in some sense two names for the same process. Some sense of that has always made me mistrust Samuel Taylor Coleridge's famous take-down (in *Biographia Literaria*) of "fancy" (etymologically of course an abbreviation of "fantasy")—"no other than a mode of Memory emancipated from the order of time and space"—as inferior to true "imagination," "a repetition in the finite mind of the eternal act of creation in the infinite I AM" (1.305, 304). Coleridge's own terminology undermines him, for it's really a matter of choosing between two terms, Greek or Latin, which mean the same thing: "imagination," from Latin *imaginare*, to form an image of; "fantasy," from Greek *phantasia*, a making visible, ultimately from *phainein*, to show.

I don't think I've gone very far astray here. There's nothing amiss in indulging in a bit of etymological talmudizing when discussing Norman Finkelstein's poetry, for that poetry has always been invested in processes of textual interpretation—the simultaneously exfoliating and hermeneutic traditions of Jewish scriptural commentary, the interminable psychic archaeologies of Freudian analysis. From *Track*:

> In some versions
> there are many versions
> and in some versions only one
>
> around which the commentators
> weave endless versions
> as if to explain. (*Ratio* 105)

And, a decade and a half later, from *From the Files of the Immanent Foundation*:

> In one version the space must be opened
> and in another version the space
> must be closed. And in the explanation,
>
> a space either opens or closes,
> producing yet another version.
> In one version there is a storyteller

and in another version there is a scholar.
And in the explanation, the scholar speaks
to the storyteller and explains all the versions. (*Ratio* 308)

But if the poet Finkelstein is a textualist, an interpreter, a tunneler through layers of texts both literal and psychic—"a prophet turned archaeologist, / a scribe turned into a scribe" (*Ratio* 204)—the title of his selected poems, *The Ratio of Reason to Magic*, gestures toward just as deep an investment in fantastika, as Clute defines it. Finkelstein's work has been punctuated from the beginning with traces of the fantastic, allusion to various canonical works of fantastika. In his first full collection, *Restless Messengers* (1992), we find such poems as "A Poem for the Little Shoemakers" and "Hans My Hedgehog" (drawing on the Brothers Grimm), "The Great God Pan" (playing off Kenneth Grahame's *The Wind in the Willows*), and "A Poem for the Erl King" (echoing Goethe's uncanny ballad). In *Scribe* (2009), two poems ("For Count Zero" and "Western World" ["after *Idoru*"]) allude to novels by the Canadian-American science fiction author William Gibson. Finkelstein's collections are peppered with overt allusions to texts of fantastika: the contemporary fantasy authors John Crowley ("Ægypt," "Appointment" [which refers to the novel *Little, Big*]) and China Miéville (whose horrific "grindylow" from *The Scar* appear in "Novel"), but also Arthur Machen, J. R. R. Tolkien, H. P. Lovecraft, Ursula K. Le Guin, and I'm sure a host of others. As significantly, Finkelstein's poetry continually moves between the registers of the quotidian and the supernatural, the realm of the everyday and a realm that transcends the everyday. He represents poetry itself, that is, not merely as a kind of "clarifying" of experience—what we may take as one definition of the Objectivist project—but as itself a sort of "magic."

Let's try another bout with the sorting hat, another round of my categorizing fancies. If we take Finkelstein as a member of some roughly defined "group"—perhaps the "New Gnostic" poets, including Joseph Donahue, Peter O'Leary, Patrick Pritchett, Nathaniel Mackey— might we read the presence of extra-realistic elements in their work— Donahue's and Pritchett's work are shot through with supernaturalism;

Mackey's vast ongoing *Song of the Andoumboulou* is a kind of dream-journey that recalls George MacDonald's and William Morris's romance; and most outrageously, O'Leary has recently published *The Sampo*, a full-scale work of heroic narrative fantasy in verse—as indicating some profound affinity between the "New Gnosticism" and fantasy? (Note how, like an plodding literary historian, I have moved from the adjectival to the nominalized form.) And not merely "fantasy" as anti-realistic imaginative mode, but fantasy in its more modern, narrow generic sense? Or is it simply an index of these writers' adolescent (and post-adolescent) reading?

Or perhaps, more outrageously, should we consider O'Leary's *The Sampo* and much of Finkelstein's work—certainly *Inside the Ghost Factory* and *From the File of the Immanent Foundation*—as in some sense "fantasy poetry"? In my own critical peregrinations, I have been doing some genre-switching of late, spending some time in the strange and unfamiliar provinces of fantasy "genre" criticism. It's an odd but rich world, its critical discourses sometimes canted at an alarming degree athwart those we find in the more "mainstream" realm of the Modern Language Association. They don't talk much about poetry at fantasy/science fiction conferences: Yes, there are occasional papers on *The Faerie Queene* or William Morris's narrative poems, but in general there's a pretty pervasive absence of discussion of contemporary poetry.

To explain this fully would require a potted history of popular literature from the nineteenth century on, the general displacement of poetry as a popular genre by prose fiction and its elevation (or relegation) to "literary" or "high culture" status. Suffice it to say that what gets written and promoted as "fantasy poetry" is usually *genre* verse, like "cowboy" poetry or adolescent romantic poetry: a poetry written either in traditional forms or in slack free verse, meant to be read not for its intensity of linguistic engagement but for its narrative or descriptive content—elves, unicorns, and starships in stanzas, rather than paragraphs.

The fantastic is at the very base of the western poetic tradition. One need only mention the great narrative long poems that traffic in the supernatural: the *Iliad*, the *Odyssey*, *The Faerie Queene* and *Paradise*

Lost, all of them central to any poetic canon, can be read as works of fantastika. It's true that most of the "literary" poetry published in the twentieth and twenty-first centuries (and I think the uncomfortable pleonasm of that phrase "'literary' poetry"—compare "literary fiction," which sounds quite familiar—underscores the literary-historical divide to which I've just alluded) has been content to inhabit a region we might call the "quotidian realistic." But we're still quite accustomed to "serious" poets veering into moments of fantastika: witness the ghosts and fairies of Yeats's work; the Ovidian metamophoses and transfigurations of *The Cantos* and *The Waste Land;* the phantasmagoria of Wallace Stevens; the very different psychic communications of Hannah Weiner and James Merrill; the shifting realities—alternately George Macdonald and Philip K. Dick—of Robert Duncan, Ronald Johnson, Nathaniel Mackey.

There is evident here, I think, a basic categorical difference in the ways that we receive and categorize prose fiction and poetry. In prose narrative, fantasy, science fiction, and associated genres—Fantastika, in short—has generally been identified by its deviations from the canons of a hegemonic realist tradition. In poetry, however, a mode of writing usually distinguished by its *formal* characteristics, strictures of realism have a far more tenuous influence. It is the freedom of the poet to range like Coleridge from the convalescent's lime-tree bower to the Mariner's haunted polar seas, like Keats from Hampstead, London to "faery lands forlorn," like Eliot from a typist's sordid apartment to Parsifal's Grail chapel, like Yeats from the tumult of the Irish Civil War to a vast sphinx-like "image out of Spiritus Mundi" stirring in the desert, like Stevens from the ice-shagged trees of a Connecticut winter to the Palace of Hoon—without leaving the realm of poetry.

In the context of a discussion of Finkelstein's poetry, this talmudizing about genre serves little purpose other than to underscore what I've always taken as one of the strongest characteristics of this work, which is precisely its resistance to categorization: is Finkelstein a realist or a fantasist? is he a modernist? a post-modernist? a romantic? a post-Objectivist? Perhaps one can only answer, yes. And if we take it as axiomatic that one of the primary modes of Finkelstein's work is, well, talmudizing—that is, the hermeneutic or commentarial—and another is the fantastic, we can ask what role precisely does fantastika play in the overall movement of his poetry? What are those goblins, trolls, wizards, and grindylows doing?

The poet George Oppen, one of Finkelstein's central influences, in his poem "Route" utters a striking paean to what one might take as a "realistic" poetic:

> Clarity, clarity, surely clarity is the most beautiful thing in the world,
> A limited, limiting clarity
>
> I have not and never did have any motive of poetry
> But to achieve clarity (*New Collected Poems* 193)

One of the "ghost voices" in *Inside the Ghost Factory* speaks a sentence which, even as it parodies Oppen, seems to encapsulate much of Finkelstein's own poetics: "I have not and never did have any motive of poetry / but to move between codes" (*Ratio* 284). "Codes" evokes the hermeneutic; it's in the "moving" that the interest lies, the shifting, switching, leaping from one thing to another. Finkelstein's is a poetry of code-switching,[3] of constant "free movements / between the realms" (333)—between realms, over stretches of unknowing, of darkness, of unspeakable and eldritch threat. The figure for that space between is of course the "abyss": "Gone into the abyss / the wizard and his foe," (184) Finkelstein writes in *Track*, evoking at once Gandalf's struggle with the Balrog on the bridge of Khazad-Dûm (*The Fellowship of the Ring*) and the wizard Ged at the climax of Le Guin's *The Farthest Shore*.

And then there is the more everyday "abyss" the poet confronts with each attempt at composition, the gulf that must be leaped—or fallen into—with every movement from sentence to sentence, line to line, as Finkelstein muses in "Collage (in memory of Helen Adam)." "What is found in the passage between?" he asks; "It is there, I suppose, that the 'magic' is to be found, if it is to be found anywhere at all." (214) The title *The Ratio of Reason to Magic* names the ambivalence with

---

3. Finkelstein himself evokes this term in his notes to *From the Files of the Immanent Foundation* (*Ratio* 359).

which Finkelstein regards the fantastic, measured as it always is against the rational, the "reasonable." At one point in *Track* he would dismiss fantastika in favor of the more prosaic "mystery":

> Nor is language magic
> as in some cabal
> waving their wands
>
> Not magic but mystery
> into which one may go (*Ratio* 187)

But I take this as a distinction without any real difference. What are the Eleusinian Mysteries, so central to Ezra Pound's and Robert Duncan's notions of what is "modern" in poetry, but rites of *magic?*

The "magic" of poetry, and the poetry of magic, lies in its ability at once to evoke and to leap over psychic abysses, depths inhabited or haunted by fantastic beasts more threatening than Rowling's Dementors or Tolkien's Ringwraiths. And here it's time to introduce a lapidary sentence from the late Antony Easthope's 1989 study *Poetry and Phantasy:* "There is now no alternative," Easthope writes, "to reading literature in some relation to psychoanalysis, a fact increasingly recognized among most of those concerned with literary study" (3). Easthope wears his fantasy with a difference, the "Ph" with which he spells it signaling that it should be taken not in the generic but in the Freudian sense, as "an imaginary scene or narrative ... altered and disguised so that it may fulfil a wish for the subject" (11). Poems, Easthope argues—and this is central to his Marxist-psychoanalytic project—are social phantasies, "shared symbolic expression[s]" (43) thoroughly embedded in the historical and ideological moments of both their production and their reception.

Finkelstein's monsters, then, those dwellers in the abyss which he evokes with the shorthand of fantastika—Lovecraft's "monsters of Providence" (280), Miéville's terrifying grindylow ("She hears the rattle of bones as the necklace / of the grindylow magus shakes with each flicker / of his tail" [338]), and so many others—are the monsters that lurk beneath our everyday lives: the terrifying and disruptive drives that Freud identified as the occluded motors of our individual psyches. But they are as well all the forces that bear us onward, upward, and downward, the monsters of class struggle, ideology, socio-economic change, and *history* in general, whose inchoate and ghastly lineaments we are only able to glimpse in momentary flashes, like a shoggoth down a distant tunnel.

Recall the magus-poet of Coleridge's "Kubla Khan"—"Beware! Beware! / His flashing eyes, his floating hair!" (one of Finkelstein's ghost-voices snorts, "Floating hair, right? To think / it has come to this" [*Ratio* 273]). The wizard is one but only one figure for the poet in Finkelstein's work: indeed, a composite Finkelstein-poet, in my own imagination—or fancy—would be a combination of Doctor Strange, Sigmund Freud, a Talmudic scholar, and some hapless mid-level Kafkaesque bureaucrat, daily turning over files that hint at troubling secrets far above his pay grade.

Poetry as fantastika can evoke the shoggoths and the grindylows; but the fantastic in Finkelstein's writing also stands as an emblem of poetry's ability to transform and transfigure experience, both deep and immediately present, both the remembered and the textual past, to speak it and therefore—in a kind of "talking cure"—to come to (uncertain, provisional) terms with it. We name and create fantastic monsters, fantastic plights, fantastic bureaucratic entanglements—the emblems of "neurotic misery," to quote one of Finkelstein's rabbis—to embody and in some sense confront the elements of our "real" existence, to restore us to "ordinary unhappiness." The poem, like Aaron's transmogrifying rod in that second book of fantasy, is a transformative wizard's staff, one of the aramentarium of miracles that might deliver us from Egypt—or Ægypt, or "Egyptomania" (*Ratio* 359–60)—if not to a promised land, then to our own trackless but intermittently hopeful wilderness.

Works Cited

Benjamin, Walter. "Unpacking My Library: A Talk About Collecting." Trans. Harry Zohn. *Selected Writings, Volume 2: 1927–1934*. Ed. Michael W. Jennings. Cambridge, MA: Belknap/Harvard UP, 1999. 486–93.

Roger Chartier, *The Order of Books: Readers, Authors, and Libraries in Europe Between the 14th and 18th Centuries*. Trans. Lydia G. Cochrane. Stanford: Stanford UP, 1994.

Clute, John. "Fantastika." *The Encyclopedia of Science Fiction*. http://www.sf-encyclopedia.com/entry/fantastika.

Coleridge, Samuel Taylor. *Biographia Literaria; or, Biographical Sketches of My Literary Life and Opinions*. 2 vols. Ed. James Engell and W. Jackson Bate. Princeton, NJ: Princeton UP, 1983.

Delany, Samuel R., "About 5.750 Words," *The Jewel-Hinged Jaw: Notes on the Language of Science Fiction*. New York: Berkley, 1977. 21–37.

Finkelstein, Norman. *Inside the Ghost Factory*. East Rockaway, New York: Marsh Hawk, 2010.

———. *The Ratio of Reason to Magic: New and Selected Poems*. Loveland, OH: Dos Madres, 2015.

———. *Restless Messengers*. Athens, GA: U of Georgia P, 1992.

———. *Scribe*. Loveland, OH: Dos Madres, 2009.

Alastair Fowler. *Kinds of Literature: An Introduction to the Theory of Genres and Modes*. Cambridge, MA: Harvard UP, 1982.

Jameson, Fredric. *Archaeologies of the Future: The Desire Called Utopia and Other Science Fictions*. London: Verso, 2005.

O'Leary, Peter. *The Sampo*. Brooklyn: The Cultural Society, 2016.

Oppen, George. *New Collected Poems*. Ed. Michael Davidson. New York: New Directions, 2002.

Williamson, Jamie. *The Evolution of Modern Fantasy: From Antiquarianism to the Ballantine Adult Fantasy Series*. New York: Palgrave Macmillan, 2015.

We Entered By the Middle Gate: An Open Letter to Norman Finkelstein on the Poetics of Collective Experience

Robert Archambeau

"Dear J," "Dear K," "Dear M," begin some of the lines in Norman Finkelstein's long poem, or series of poems, or agglomeration of poetic acts, called *Track*. And I'm taking that as authorization to begin this essay with "Dear N," or "Dear N.F.," or (why not?) "Dear Norman."

Dear Norman:

Who—who exactly—do you think you are?

I ask because I'm not sure you know. Or at least, I'm not sure the you of, say, the 1990s knows who you would become. It was back then that you were writing most of the essays that went into your collection *Lyrical Interference*, and the Norman Finkelstein who wrote that book was a bit skeptical about the erasure of the lyric self, or lyric ego, from poetry. You remember him, I'm sure—the young Norman? He was the man who plucked the phrase "lyrical interference" from Olson's "Projective Verse" for his title—and did so not so much to praise Olson as to bury him (or at least to bury a bit of his poetics). Olson had written of poetry "getting rid of the lyrical interference of the individual as ego, of the 'subject' and his soul" (Olson 24). Young Norman took issue with this, not only as a goal, but as a possibility—the individual ego could not, claimed the young Finkelstein in *Lyrical Interference*, "be so easily jettisoned" (9).

Yes, the individual ego is with us ever. But what would 1990s

Finkelstein think of the relative erasure of the individual ego from so
many of the works he was to write in the decades to come? Were he to
ask the Finkelstein of the later period who he was, the first answer he'd
come to by consulting the poetry would be something like "he doesn't
think he's an ego, an 'I,' at all—he thinks he's a 'we,' an 'us.'" And I don't
mean some Whitmanic self who encompasses all, some Wordsworthian
egotistical sublime. I mean something different, something less ego-
centered and more collective—even to the point of a transcendental
or mystic dissolution of the self into something greater. "Who do you
think you are?" I ask (along with my imagined 1990s Finkelstein).
"Wrong question" comes the response.

Let's begin with pronouns. For a poet who once set out to defend
the lyrical presence in poetry, you've been putting very few first person
singular pronouns into play (in fact, one signature device has been to
write without pronouns, or any other indication of the grammatical
subject—here, for example, are a couple of sections from the poem
"Desert." Party game: count the grammatical subjects!

5.
Called back, returned, and so went forth
again. From the edge of the abyss, "the
deep places of the imagination," retrieved,
rescued, redeemed. Fronted, confronted,
conspired, conspired against, usurped,
stolen, sacrificed. Bidden, forbidden.
Dreamed, prophesied, spoke to, with,
against. Visited, was visited
upon. Throned. Dethroned. Written
upon the sky and upon the ground.

6.
Neither upon the sky nor upon the ground

Neither in the desert nor at the mountain

Neither in the heights nor in the depths

Neither present nor absent

Neither known nor unknown

Neither strange nor familiar

Neither whole nor in fragments

Neither revealed nor hidden

Neither sacred nor profane

Neither spoken nor silent. (*The Ratio of Reason to Magic* 229)

Neither, one might add, a lyrical ego nor a pronominal subject. Elsewhere in the poem we do get a subject—a subject named "no one"—"No one climbing these peaks;/no one guided by this pillar of flame" and so forth. This nonentity is hardly an individuated, expressive, lyric self.

The sample I offer is by no means an exception. If we take *Scribe*, the book from which "Desert" comes, we find very little by way of the first person singular. Go through the poems and you'll see: "Like Dates and Almonds, Purple Cloth and Pearls," uses a collective "we," as does "Threshold." The title poem uses a plural "you," "Lamp" uses "we," "For Count Zero" uses "he" and "she," "Drones and Chants" is all about "they." Even "Valentine," a love poem, where we might expect an "I" to appear, praises the red-haired beloved without ever invoking the first person lover (it's all "he" and "she"). We do get an "I" in "Collage," but it's a persona, writing a letter, and one who soon starts speaking of how "we" undertook collective research.

Nor is *Scribe* an exception among your mature works in this regard. Consider these lines from *Columns* (itself a part of the larger work *Track*):

> Speaking to the dead
> for the dead
>
> Speaking of speaking
> to or for the dead
>
> Speaking what was
> whispered in secret
>
> Speaking the whispers
> of or in the clouds.

Your fellow Gnostic, the poet Peter O'Leary, correctly calls this a "characteristic" passage of *Columns* (n.p.), and one way it is characteristic of both that work and of your later period poetry is in the absence of a subject for those verbs. You don't write "I am speaking," here, you give us, instead, a subjectless act of speech.

For a sense of the significance of your characteristic anti-lyrical or anti-egocentric gesture, we can turn to Michael Palmer. It was he, after all, who said that to read *Scribe* was "to pass through a series of gates into the paradoxical heart of the poem," where "the communal and the solitary" come together in the music of the poetry (n.p.). He was on to something, I think: what strikes one most strongly in *Scribe* are the repeated invocations of communal experience, and the ways the influence on collectivity works its way into the forms, as well as the subjects, of the poetry.

We don't get past the first word of the first poem before we feel that we're entering a meditation on collective experience: "Like Dates and Almonds, Purple Cloth and Pearls," the poem that opens the first of *Scribe*'s three parts, begins with the collective, plural pronoun:

> We entered by the middle gate
> because the first gate frightened us
> with the ox and the pit, the destruction and the fire.
> We were old men and we were children

old men disguised as children
long ago and yesterday and the day after tomorrow. (*Ratio* 201)

By the time we're through to the end of the stanza, we're not just on a physical journey together—we've entered into a kind of community over time, bound to the distant past and the future. As we read on, it becomes clear that we are bound in this community less by the experience of a shared journey than by the experience of common texts or stories:

We dreamed of it and spoke of it
dreamed that we spoke of it
spoke of it and wrote of it
upon parchments of deerskin.
With the meat we fed the orphans
and on the skins wrote the five books
and took the books to the city
where there were no teachers
and taught five children the five books
and six children the six orders
and told them: We shall return
but in the meantime let each of you
teach this book and all his order to the others. (*Ratio* 201)

What we're seeing, here, is nothing less than the evolution of the Torah—the five books of Moses—and the Mishnah, or Shisha Sedarim, the six orders into which the oral version of the Torah was first edited and compiled. This compiling, of course, opened up the long, ongoing tradition of commentary, redaction, and interpretation that binds the Jewish people together, through dispersal over space and time, as a people of the book.

Significantly, the poem goes on to tell us that the process of passing on these texts involves "nothing like nostalgia." There's no desire to keep a pure ur-text here, no desire to return to a lost authoritative story. Rather, we see that the process of passing on the textual tradition is "like a word twisted into a ring / and like a ring lost in a deep pool / and like a ring found in the belly of a fish / so it might return to the sea." What you value, Norman, are the transformations, metamorphoses, and miraculous recontextualizations of a tradition as it travels through time. The proliferation of interpretations and the evolution of reconfigured texts aren't sources of conflict, in this view: they are signs of a living tradition, and a rich, collective conversation.

Your friend Michael Heller once wrote of Louis Zukofsky as having an acute sense of "the Jew's particular burden of aloneness," and argued that his poetic reinscriptions of "family history, religion, philosophy, and poetic tradition" arose out of this burden of solitude (165). We certainly find a strong web of community spun from a sense of traditions inscribed and re-inscribed in your work. Indeed, the feeling is less of aloneness, but of a (possibly compensatory) loss of self in something far grander and more enduring than the individual ego. In an unlikely and perhaps roundabout way, we may even think of your work as representing, in certain respects, a fulfillment of the ideal of the mature poet as outlined in T. S. Eliot's famous essay "Tradition and the Individual Talent." Do you not share something, after all, with the writer of a phrase like "the progress of an artist is a continual self-sacrifice, a continual extinction of personality" (n.p.)? Perhaps you don't share Eliot's martyr complex, but certainly you share with him the downplaying of individual lyric subjectivity. And not only that: you share with him something like the related notion of tradition (which fills the void once inhabited by the subject) as an evolving, living entity, not repeated but modified (to steal from Auden) in the guts of the living:

> ... if the only form of tradition, of handing down, consisted in following the ways of the immediate generation before us in a blind or timid adherence to its successes, "tradition" should positively be discouraged.... [Tradition] involves, in the first place, the historical sense, which we may call nearly indispensable to any one who would continue to be a poet beyond his twenty-fifth year; and the historical sense involves a perception, not only of the pastness of the past, but of its presence.... ("Tradition and the Individual Talent" n.p.)

Scribe certainly gives us this sense of the presence of the past, and of lives lived (as Eliot puts it) "in what is not merely the present, but the present moment of the past" (n.p.). We see this most clearly when, in *Scribe's* title poem, we witness an enactment of the kind of reconfiguration of source-texts we saw praised in "Like Dates and Almonds, Purple Cloth and Pearls."

The eponymous poem is addressed to us (that is, to the second person, to a "you" with whom readers are invited to identify) by an unknown speaker, and describes "our" experiences in a world that is best described as a free-style reinterpretation of Old Testament symbols, events, and settings. Here, we experience ourselves as drifting through a morphed-yet-still-recognizable world, a world made from the free reinterpretation of traditional text. When we arrive at the end of the poem, we are told "you have heeded the word of the outside god / and you have heeded the word of no god at all, / like a prophet turned archaeologist, / a scribe turned into a scribe" (*Ratio* 204). In these lines you draws our attention to our distance from the people who first experienced the events recounted in the Old Testament: we cannot enter into the consciousness of pre-modern prophets any more than they could enter into the scientific consciousness of an archaeologist, even though both types of person are concerned with the same tradition. But he also draws our attention to our continuity with the past, to the modern persistence of the role of scribe as preserver, commentator, and re-arranger of traditional text. In the end, we share an identity with the past, even as we are distanced from it: we are in the past, to be sure, but in its present moment, together.

The second of the book's sections is devoted to collaged text and epistolary poetry, both forms of collective creativity. Here, Norman, you don't simply celebrate collective creativity (not that there was anything simple in the celebration). In "At the Threshold," for example, you address the difficult question of imaginative sympathy for a person who would not return that sympathy. The threshold imagery that runs through the poem is clearly drawn from Heidegger's thinking, particularly his writing on the poet Georg Trakl. One can certainly understand the appeal of Heidegger to a poet like you, with his concerns about language revealing and concealing different elements of the truth over time. But of course you know the question of Heidegger's Nazism cannot be shunted aside, especially not for a poet so deeply rooted in the Jewish tradition. So you don't deny yourself the experience of thinking-through, and thinking-with, Heidegger, but you clearly recognize (in yet another invocation of the collective "we") that to do so requires a special suspension of historical realities, in which people must act:

> As if we
> Too had drunk
> At the star-well
>
> As if we
> Were with him on
> The way to language
>
> Yellow stars
> In a black forest (*Ratio* 220–221)

I don't know what's more resonant here, the line "The way to language," which brings to mind the title of Heidegger's *Unterwegs zur Sprache*, or the image of the "Yellow Stars / In a black forest," a haunting double vision of the symbol the Nazis forced Jews to wear, and of the Black Forest near Heidegger's hut at Todnauberg.

The third and longest part of *Scribe* consists of poems that quote from, and riff on, passages from architect Christopher Alexander's famous book on traditional design, *A Pattern Language*. Here, again, we see an emphasis on collectivity. As you say in an endnote to the book, you were first drawn to *A Pattern Language* because of that book's "idea of community," of architecture as an art of the social world (110). Many of the poems discuss the idea of community in urban and domestic spaces, but it is at the level of form that ideas of community and collective creativity come into full flower: the poems read less like your private thoughts than as a series of annotations and elaborations on substantial quotations from Alexander's writing. The feeling one gets is akin to that of reading scribal commentaries on a traditional text:

there is a kind of collaboration at work, as a source text is elaborated and grows in meaning.

You've spoken of *Scribe* as representing the rhapsodic side of your work—and I understand. But there's little of the aching individual, of the stereotypically Romantic *I* at play. Like the more recent poems of *From the Files of the Immanent Foundation* (where the most common gesture is an invitation), the most common subject is plural, a collective 'we' into which all of us are taken up. This is enormously significant: the gesture of your work isn't inward but, to kidnap Donald Revell's words about your writing, it is a matter of "motions outward; an outstretched hand" (5).

I'd sign my name to this letter, except that seems out of keeping with the collective spirit that dominates so much of your poetry. So let me end, instead, by saying we appreciate you. All of us.

Works Cited

Eliot, T.S. "Tradition and the Individual Talent." The Poetry Foundation. https://www.poetryfoundation.org/articles/69400/tradition-and-the-individual-talent

Finkelstein, Norman. *Lyrical Interference: Essays on Poetics.* New York: Sputen Duyvil, 2004.

———. *The Ratio of Reason to Magic: New and Selected Poems.* Loveland, Ohio: Dos Madres, 2016.

Heller, Michael. *Uncertain Poetries: Selected Essays on Poets, Poetry and Poetics.* Bristol, UK: Shearsman, 2012.

O'Leary, Peter. Review of *Track* by Norman Finkelstein. *The Volta* (October 1, 2013). http://www.thevolta.org/inreview-track.html

Olson, Charles. *Selected Writings.* New York: New Directions, 1971.

Palmer, Michael. Cover copy. *Scribe*, by Norman Finkelstein. Loveland, Ohio: Dos Madres, 2009.

Revell, Donald. "Introduction." *Lyrical Interference: Essays on Poetics,* by Norman Finkelstein. New York: Sputen Duyvil, 2004: 5–7.

Where the Heart Is: Toward a Heymish Reading of Norman Finkelstein

Eric Murphy Selinger

In an autobiographical essay from 1996, Norman Finkelstein described his way of thinking as "volatile and dialectical" ("The Master of Turning," 117). The poet's nearly forty-year career has, indeed, been marked by a series of stylistic swerves and dynamic tensions: the writing of both poetry and literary criticism; within the criticism, the writing of both rigorous scholarship and reflective, musing poetics; within the poetry, the writing of both Romantic lyrics and serial postmodern fragments; and within each of these poetries, the writing of what one might call "argument poems," whether these are structured in the form of dialogic argument or of paratactic clashes.[1] In the title of Finkelstein's New and Selected Poems, *The Ratio of Reason to Magic*, we find yet another opposition: a pair of terms in mathematical relation that have now been given pride of place as the Blakean "contraries" that structure Finkelstein's literary work as an evolving, self-elaborating whole.

These are, of course, resonant and useful terms. They conjure up, respectively, the spirits of Romance ("magic" echoes Yeats and Duncan) and of an astringent and demystifying clarity ("reason" nods to Zukofsky and Freud). In the spirit of contrariety, however, I would propose that neither "magic" nor "reason" quite gets at the wellsprings of pleasure in Finkelstein's work. Instead of these, or alongside them, I want to propose a reading focused on the dialectical exchanges between things like Sentiment and Disaffection, Restlessness and Comfort, Familiarity and Estrangement (or perhaps Unsettlement). Much of Finkelstein's work is engaged in a project of building a textual "world elsewhere" in which the reader—at least a certain sort of reader—can take refuge, and even when this world is disrupted or abandoned, as at the start of Finkelstein's long poem *Track*, the oscillations of his

---

1. For an account of Finkelstein and the poetics of Jewish argument, see my essay "Azoy Toot a Yid: Secular Poetics and 'The Jewish Way,'" especially pp. 364–372.

work bring us back, again and again, to a "realm" or "room" or "street café" or "temple" or guarded "heart": a literal, metaphorical, and / or theological place that we repair *to* (a verb that comes from *re-patriare*, meaning to return to one's home country, to the *patria*) so that we may be, ourselves, *repaired* (a verb derived from *re-parāre*, meaning to make something ready again or put it back in order.). With both senses in mind, we might think of Finkelstein's work as enacting a *reparative* poetics, a term that perhaps allows his work to resonate with what Eve Kosofsky Sedgwick famously dubbed "reparative reading"—the sort by which "selves and communities succeed in extracting sustenance from the objects of a culture—even of a culture whose avowed desire has often been not to sustain them" (150–151). More colloquially, we might say that his work is profoundly *heymish*, and before returning to Sedgwick, this *heymishkeyt* needs to be explored.

Uriel Weinreich's "Modern English-Yiddish Yiddish-English Dictionary" translates "heymish" as "cozy ... familiar, intimate, informal" (638). In *The Joys of Yiddish*, Leo Rosten elaborates. "Heymish," he tells us, means "the opposite of snobbish, supercilious, or, to get fancy about it, charismatic." A person or thing that is heymish has "the friendly characteristics, or kind of rapport, that exist inside a happy home" (145), and of course the word is a cognate of the German *heim*—the root of *das unheimlich*, the Freudian uncanny. When columnist David Brooks deployed the word *heymish* to describe the safari camps he liked on a family trip to Africa, a more recent popular Yiddishist, Michael Wex, took the opportunity to elaborate still further. "The original sense of heymish," Wex writes, "'involves an appeal to a shared Jewish culture that transcends ideological borders. It reflects a time when communists and chasidim spoke the same language, hungered for the same sorts of dishes and conducted the same kinds of arguments, albeit about vastly different topics" ("The Heymish Safari"). By extension, then, *heymishkayt* "goes deeper than the *gemütlichkeit* of the safaris' hired help," because it "evokes a set of shared attitudes and assumptions that are thought to lie beyond—or even beneath—the religious or political differences of people who speak the same *mameloshen*, or mother tongue, who spent their formative years suckling at the same cultural bosom. It's an almost intuitive sense of common values, an inescapable sense of common interest" ("The Heymish Safari").

Heymishkayt is not yet, as far as I know, an established term in literary theory. And yet, we do have something like it in Roland Barthes's *The Pleasure of the Text*—specifically, in Barthes's description of the "text of pleasure" as opposed to the "text of *jouissance*." The text of pleasure "contents, fills, grants euphoria" because it "comes from culture and does not break with it, is linked to a comfortable practice of reading." It stands in dynamic tension with the text of *jouissance*, the one which "imposes a state of loss," which "discomforts (perhaps to the point of a certain boredom)," and which "unsettles the reader's historical, cultural, psychological assumptions, the consistency of his tastes, values, memories, brings to a crisis his relation with language" (14). In a Jewish context, of course, Barthes' dichotomy blossoms into a complex and productive irony, since modern Jewish culture is routinely said to be profoundly unsettled, inconsistent, and in crisis: a tradition one cannot easily "break with" since it is, itself, a "tradition of rupture," in Yerushalmi's famous phrase (114). As Finkelstein glosses this idea in "A Tomb for Gershom Scholem," in Jewish culture, "The cracks *are* the edifice" (*Ratio*, 59), and much of Finkelstein's work from the 1990s can productively be read as exploring this irony.

The *heymishkeyt* of *Restless Messengers* (1992) and *Passing Over* (published in 2007, but containing poems from 1989–96) often involves a complex interplay between the poems' reassuring range of Jewish reference and their repeated articulations of some distance from or falling out with Ashkenazi culture and tradition. Angels and thieves drift in from the world of folktale; one hears musical nods to Schubert, Brahms, and the Klezmatics; the four archangels of Jewish modernism—Kafka, Freud, Scholem, and Walter Benjamin—sponsor these poems in epigraphs, while overhead one senses the sheltering presence of Reb Nachman of Breslov, at least in his recent incarnation as a modernist *avant-la-lettre*. Consider "A Poem for Storytellers":

> A handful of stories is all one has to offer
> even in seeking to remake the world.

> If the seventh beggar, the legless one,
>> could tell his tale and dance at the wedding,
>>> all would be restored.
> But the message is lost in the act of transmission
>> and the wisdom has long since decayed.
> The beautiful maiden leaves the king's court
>> and goes off on her own.
>> So the tale begins
>> but it never finds its ending,
> as the impulse is finally dissipated
>> and lost in windy silence. (*Restless Messengers* 27)

At which point, the poem stops: an abrupt and discomfiting finish, with a shiver of failure nicely captured in the hiss and dying fall of the last four lines. Yet even as one shivers, a reader (*this* reader) can tug up the blanket of knowing that these breaks in transmission are, themselves, richly traditional, with Reb Nachman's "Tale of the Seven Beggars" the poem's major source. For all that "A Poem for Storytellers" ends with "windy silence," then, one turns the page with a phrase from another text, "A Poem for Orphans," in the back of one's mind: "Be comforted, children—your loss is your own" (*Restless Messengers* 4).

The ironies of "A Poem for Storytellers" are mostly *sotto voce*, whispered in the space between the poem's assertions of loss and its comfortable (or at least comforting) transmission of Jewish tradition. Elsewhere in these volumes one hears a different, more visibly contrapuntal strain of unsettlement, distance, and argument. "They cast me from the congregation /—but they still come to hear me teach" boasts the eponymous Rabbi Elisha ben Abuya, the Other, the "Akher" (*Ratio* 62) and other voices concur. "I hover around the table, / peek from the margins of the book" the mysterious Fifth Son thus whispers in "Passing Over," Finkelstein's commentary-poem on the Passover Haggadah (*Ratio* 76); unlike the four sons named in the original text— the wise, the evil, the simple, and the one who does not know how to ask—the fifth pipes up to bless moments of displacement, indecision, and paradox.

When order is passing
into disorder
and hope is trembling like wine in a cup

seek for me
more precious than the afikoman
seek for me

so that all can be incomplete
unfinished unfinished
on both sides of the door. (*Ratio* 76)

The multiple meanings of "unfinished" here—"unfinished" in the sense of something ongoing and unending, like the "disputation without telos" of rabbinic argument (Boyarin 161); "unfinished" in the sense of an interminable analysis (Freud); "unfinished" in the sense of an artwork retaining some roughness, and thereby some trace of its making—all gesture toward the realm that Finkelstein describes near the end of the sequence as "the domain of song never completed, / not even by the Holy One, Blessed be He" (*Ratio* 93). Song, like Torah, is "לֹא בַשָּׁמַיִם" not in the heavens (Deut. 30:12), and like all things in the human realm it is marked by an irreducible, irresolvable ambivalence. As the last words of the sequence declare: "I think we want and we do not want / and that is where the recitation leads us / I think we recite and do not recite / and that is where the wanting leads us" (*Ratio* 94).

This counterpoint between comfort and unsettlement in Finkelstein's early work is a textual equivalent, I think, of Wex's historicized account of *heymishkayt*: that communal Yiddish space in which the opposite trajectories of Ashkenazi culture might still converge and converse. These poems assume—quite correctly, I believe—that a poetry skewed too far in either direction would feel far less familiar, intimate, and welcoming to the reader, or at least a certain *kind* of reader: one for whom too much distance from and too close a proximity to Jewish culture would seem equally problematic. In Sedgwick's resonant term, we might think of this "Fifth Son" or "Akherian" phase in Finkelstein's work as enacting a "reparative reading" of Jewishness: that is, the sort of reading by which "selves and communities succeed in extracting sustenance from the objects of a culture—even of a culture whose avowed desire has often been not to sustain them" (150–51). (Akher *has* been cast out of the congregation and renamed "The Other," lest we forget.) But the poet's reparative reading is not strictly or exclusively of Jewish sources. Finkelstein casts the same warm eye on the traditions of English-language poetry, especially post-Romantic poetry, as he does on anything Jewish. If I feel at home in Finkelstein's lyrics I do so in no small part because his work sets a place for Keats and Stevens and Duncan at the Sabbath or Seder table, as though as it were perfectly natural for a poem to invoke Stevens's "there was a project for the sun, and is," the Kabbalistic task of gathering "the sparks" of deity and returning them to the Divine, Mani Leyb's "I'm not a cobbler who writes, thank Heaven / But a poet who makes shoes" ("I am ..."), and John Keats's account of this mortal world as the "Valley of Soul-Making," all in a single extraordinary figure, as at the end of "A Poem for the Little Shoemakers":

> —but the sun is warming the shoemaker's shed
> and his hammer, striking the worn sole,
> seems to make the sparks fly up into the light. (*Ratio* 16)

Or as if the ritual of searching out *chametz*, for example, had no more natural idiom than the folk-song wisdom poems of Yeats, as in "Passing Over":

> There in the corner
> and on the shelf—
> what do we search for?
> bits of ourself.
>
> *White feather, white candle,*
> *and a new wooden spoon.*

Consider this bread
as something lost.
Let us be rid of it
whatever the cost.

Crumbs and ashes
and a few old tales. (Ratio 68)

The divided relationship these poems display towards Jewish material, that is to say, is triangulated and eased of its tension by reference to Romantic *poiesis*, even as this vision of *poiesis*, which is both historically and ideologically post-Christian, becomes the home for at least one version of Jewishness.

In the same essay where he dubs his thinking "volatile and dialectical," Finkelstein muses on how an interplay of Jewish and Romantic elements gave rise to his art. "My poetic identity begins with voices and with books, in public declarations and closeted reading that thrilled the impressionable child," he explains.

In my youthful imagination, the words of the Rosh Hashanah service were strangely intertwined with those of Coleridge's "Kubla Khan":

The great shofar is sounded, and a still, small voice is heard....

I would build that dome in air,
That sunny dome! those caves of ice!
And all who heard should see them there,
And all should cry, Beware! Beware!
His flashing eyes, his floating hair!

On the deepest level, poetry and prophecy, reading and ritual, were all part of the same enchantment, the same arrival at the authoritative beauty of speech. It seemed to be a truth that could be recognized on special occasions by the entire community, but could be sustained, could be lived daily in the imagination, only by the solitary devotee. ("Master," 416)

One notes the many pairs and contrasts in this passage: not only *voices / books, public / closeted, poetry / prophecy, community / solitude, and special occasions / daily life*, all in Finkelstein's prose, but also the binaries in the pair of quoted passages, including the cry of the shofar and the still, small voice, the sunny dome and caves of ice, the doubled warning to "Beware! Beware!" and so on. The reconciling concept here is likewise called two things, "enchantment" and "truth," or perhaps more precisely *three* things: those two, plus "arrival" (as in, "arrival at the authoritative beauty of speech"). It is as though truth, however singular, could only be known in transit, only recognized (re-cognized) in the mode of dialogic and even contradictory multiplicity.

When the first volume of *Track* appeared in 1999, three years after "The Master of Turning," I read it as a self-correcting, even self-chastising turn in Finkelstein's transit: not just a contradictory moment of dialogue, but a radical swerve away from the *heymish* comforts of *Restless Messengers*. The swerve made sense: at points in the earlier book the poet had already seemed wary about the limits, or at least the potential limits, of the "texts of pleasure" he had so far composed. What if, he wonders guiltily, his work depends on "a handful of slogans, / the leaking resonance of glamorous tropes, / reduced to empty shells?" ("אֱמֶת," *Restless Messengers* 50). "Listen," the speaker warns in "Shubertiade," "the *unheimlich* is rare, / we fail to recognize its approach / for homelessness has become / our native element" (29). Fears like these can't be worked through in the same style that provoked them— and, indeed, *Track* marked a "breaking of style" (in Helen Vendler's phrase) as dramatic as hearing a Schubert art-song suddenly bristle into *sprechtstimme*. Refusing too-cozy a homelessness, Finkelstein seemed to be striving to write a truly unsettled "text of *jouissance*" and thus to make a space for the truly *unheimlich* to enter.

"In these operations," Track begins,

> no single motif
> or portrait

called Emily or K
so long as the letters
arrive to be destroyed (*Track* 13)

Where Finkelstein's earlier poems speak with a shared, coherent, and richly ambivalent voice—a voice defined, and defining itself, by a reparative quarrel with earlier texts—*Track* presents us with no such "single motif / or portrait." Whenever such a portrait starts to take shape, whether of a mysterious Dickinson-like "Emily" or a clipped, Kafkaesque "K," the stabbing, paratactic textual "operations" of this poem soon abort or undercut the process. At the turn of an enjambment the most lyrical passages here yield to—or are cut off by—a flat, oracular pronouncement or a deadpan wink.

Twenty years on, Finkelstein's initial description of *Track* as a series of "operations" still strikes me a grim, self-conscious effort to chasten and, so to speak, *postmodernize* his aesthetic. Yet as the poem's first volume goes on, for every gesture that reminds us that narrative and lyricism are old fashioned pleasures, "Bric-a-brac / in the House of Language" (*Track* 34) there are several where the poet yields, if only for a moment, to his own nostalgic love of beauty, story, rhapsody, and romance. Instead of letters being destroyed and someone "dying into the work," the poem begins to offer figures like "Wolf, son of the Name" (18) and "The thief / and the bride of the thief / and the home among the trees" (18) or lists in which the poet seems to be dealing out, card by card, a sort of private tarot:

Thief   House   Forest
Music   Crown Bride
Allegory   Wolf Eden
Trees   Letters   Children

I've been there before.
I've been here before. (*Track* 24)

By stripping away the narrative or lyrical connections between these resonant nouns, Finkelstein at once acknowledges their power over him (and us) and opens a space for himself to reconfigure them—or for them to reconfigure themselves—in fresh, revelatory arrangements, even as the space itself (a "there," a "here") strikes us a place we've been before. (It's not "House of Language" in general, after all, but a *particular* House, of a *particular* Language: a still-recognizable *heym*.)

In two notebook entries from October, 2000—parts of the "Statements for *Track*" appended to the one-volume Shearsman edition—Finkelstein mulls over the relationship between this textual *heym* and the desire to conjure up the *unheimlich*, or Freudian uncanny, in his long poem project. Musing about the unexpected shifts in patterning, eruptions of "pleasure / terror," and other "small, odd moments" that signal "a making manifest or a realizing of strangeness" in *Track*, Finkelstein poses questions (*Track* 304–5). "What exactly is the nature of these uncanny incursions? What freight do they carry?" His answer is that perhaps "what we 'loveth best' reveals itself (sometimes coming from an outside, a scary event) only against or through or coming suddenly into the structure," so that these moments of strangeness are, paradoxically, moments of profound and unsettling *familiarity*. Drawing on Freud and Duncan, he concludes that "the uncanny is heimlich in its unheimlich nature, insofar as it reveals itself as the best (and therefore first) beloved" (*Track* 305): a paradox that plays out across the course of *Track*. As the poem proceeds, we stumble on islands of narrative amid the parataxis, verses of romance and consolation, moments of humor and conviviality, all of which bear a freight of love (they are what the poem's creator "loveth best") and of the "best (and therefore first) beloved," a phrase which calls to mind the maternal / erotic / iconic figure invoked by Robert Duncan's "Often I Am Permitted to Return to a Meadow": "the First Beloved / whose flowers are flames lit to the Lady"; the "Queen Under the Hill / whose hosts are a disturbance of words within words," who blends elements of Persephone, Venus (one thinks of *Tannhäuser*), and perhaps the Maiden whom Duncan would later describe, in the poem of that name, as "precedent to that Shekhinah,   She / in whom the Jew has his communion" (*Opening of the Field* 7; 27).

These moment of coherence and affection, of sentiment in

strangeness, soften the distancing blow with which *Track* begins. Far from being a set of cold-eyed "operations," that is to say, as *Track* moves forward it increasingly aspires to be "an art / of generous proportions // Expansive, / hospitable / but measured withal // Housed in / and housing / a world" (*Track* 184). Gestures of love and intimations of romance thread through the work, as the poet stops to conjure both erotic and domestic spaces.[2] "*We'll build in sonnets pretty rooms*," Finkelstein quotes from Donne's "Canonization" and the poem is replete with homes and houses, chambers and gardens, which are as much lovers' retreats as they are figures for the poem itself as a World Elsewhere. We also find multiple gestures towards a more mysterious sense of "place," as at the start of *Powers,* the poem's third section:

> This is the place
> where strangeness ends
>
> The place forever
> folding in upon itself
>
> Which those already
> at home call home
>
> And those without rest
> can never know
>
> [...]
>
> Something taking place
> standing in place
>
> Folded in place
> and left standing

---

2. Near the end of "Woodpaths, Obscure," Mark Scroggins touches on the deployment of romantic love in some "luminous" and "consoling" moments in the first section of *Track* (212).

75

A moving place
never left behind

Wings folded
around that place (*Track* 210)

In recursive and recombinant passages like these, Finkelstein counts on his readers' sustaining a double or triple sense of a talismanic word (in this case, "place") so that they resonate together, more or less harmoniously: "place" as in the virtual space of the poem; "place" as in "The place," HaMakom, a Hebrew euphemism for the God who is "the place of the world," although "the world is not his place" (*Bereshit Rabbah* 68:10; the phrase is quoted in *Track* 103); thus, by extension, the "moving place" of the Ark of the Covenant where the cherubim's wings enfold the idol-free mercy seat ("that place" where God's Presence, the Shekhinah, resides); and, perhaps, "place" as in the Talmudic use of "that place" (*oto makom*), as euphemism for female genitalia (see, for example, *Nedarim* 20a). The place invoked, however discreetly covered, thus suggests something physical and immaterial; divine and erotic; and, within the erotic, both a female "first beloved's" body and the mother's, as an original home.

The pleasures of *Track*—or, in Barthes's terms, of reading *Track* as a "text of pleasure"—often entail such moments of recognition, whether of the cultural resonances of particular words or the more literal, even autobiographical overtones of phrases, lines, and stanzas. *Track* is, among other things, a compendium of quotations and gracious gestures: we hear quoted passages from Allen Mandelbaum's *Chelmaxioms*, Ronald Johnson's *Ark*, and other long poems of the sacred about which Finkelstein has written at length in prose; a wistful "*Wish / the Scholar-Translator were here*" (*Track* 214) brings Armand Schwerner's *The Tablets* into the mix; it is, he writes in *Track: Columns*, "As if no words / could ever be my own," the poet obliged to act as a spy "upon the lands of others" (a phrase which calls to his mind not only the Biblical spies sent to scout the promised land but Goethe's "*Kennst du das Land*," which the poem soon quotes in *fraktur* blackletter type).

To echo Wex once more on *heymishkeit*, these gestures articulate the range of reference that makes up the long poem's *mameloshen*—that is, they gesture toward a set of commonalities that the reader either already shares, or is invited to share in order to draw up a seat at the table.

I don't want to overstate the *heymishness* of *Track*. As its title suggests, *Track* is above all a book of transit, and the moments I dwell on serve as oases or moments of recuperation, rather than constancies. In another of the "Statements for *Track*," this one roughly contemporary with the publication of the second volume, *Columns*, and the writing of the third, Finkelstein touches on a similar metaphor. "The trajectory of the final volume," he writes, will be "an approach to or attempt to establish a home, a pleroma, which is a resting place in all senses of the term, which is also an uncovering or excavation of what had been such—thus simultaneously anticipatory and retrospective" (*Track* 308). If "a home" is "a pleroma" it is a place not only of familiarity, but of divine (or Gnostic) *fullness*; if it is a "resting place in all senses of the term" it is both the site of respite and a place where we rest in peace, at once the first and final home, always lost ("a loss of something ever felt I," as Dickinson says) and always still to come (to look back for home is to be "looking oppositely / For the site of the Kingdom of Heaven"). In *Track*, at least, this attempted approach will always provoke an avoidance; it will be "broken, ruptured by the immediate, the exigency of the present, in a movement that is a work of mourning and an attempt to get one's bearings." Yet "in the end," the passage concludes, the trajectory will entail a "folding back, returning 'to the text or act of love'" (*Track* 308): a phrase which suggests that the overall progress of the book-length poem might be toward something heymish, even sentimental, even if *Track* never rests there for long.

As he composed the earlier portions of *Track*, Finkelstein began a second extended project: one originally designed to be "interspersed with the first movements" of the other long poem, yet which soon "took on a life of its own" ("let the site tell you its secrets," unpaginated). A series of lyrics written in response to Christopher Alexander's *A Pattern Language*, the poems eventually gathered as *An Assembly* serve as a stable and stabilizing *basso continuo* for the restless motion of *Track*. Gathered first as a chapbook, then as a section of *Scribe, An Assembly* is not only the high-water mark of *heymishkeyt* in Finkelstein's oeuvre, but also the work in which a comforting notion of "home" is most extensively and explicitly thematized. Across the dozen poems of the sequence, step by metonymic step, Finkelstein takes us from home as the site of love and marriage and sexual tenderness—"the poem as an idea of rest entwined / around two bodies resting entwined / all their time together" (*Scribe* 52)—to home as the domain of children and childhood, both literal and as a thing preserved into the adult play of *poiesis,* "the child and adult facing each other / across a space that is all / terror and enchantment" (*Scribe* 57). The poem will eventually make its way to other spaces, urban, solitary, and communal, but the commonality of voice and movement across the sequence implicitly links these worlds of wilder play and "civic utterance" to the literally *heimish* realm where it began (*Scribe* 63). (There are, we might say, no separate spheres in the *Assembly* universe.)

In the intimate, delicate tribute to Robert Duncan that makes up "Children's Home," part five of his 2004 sequence *An Assembly,* Finkelstein writes that the older poet's work "has always been / a safe haven for me" (*Scribe* 58). In a rare, extended first-person passage, Finkelstein muses that he "go[es] into" Duncan's poetry "as a child / seeking / 'a second family,'" and the refuge he finds there seems to lie in Duncan's ability to generate doubles and opposites (e.g., a family and a second family) and then reconcile or harmonize them, so that rather than being dialectically opposed, they can sentimentally bound up in another. In Duncan, he writes, "the strange hermeneutic / passage between adult and child" stays visible; from Duncan, the apprentice poet can learn that "the work / was actually play"; to Duncan, to any student's delight, "the teacher / was also a mage"—or, to be precise, a mage whose "questing powers" have brought about an "awaited return" (*Scribe* 58). Duncan's iconic figure for the place to which one returns is, of course, the *meadow,* an "eternal pasture folded in all thought" (*Opening* 7), but Finkelstein avoids this image, turning instead to domestic and architectural imagery to round out this section of the sequence. Duncan's poetry offers him "a low wall" to sit on, "talking to passers-by," he writes: a set of "rooms and open spaces" surrounding "a common / place at the heart / / to which I return" (*Scribe* 59).

To isolate "place at the heart" as Finkelstein does in the Duncan memorial is, to me, a striking decision. Just for a moment, his poetry seems like a raid, not on the inarticulate, but on the sentimental; it is as though a well-timed enjambment could rescue this sequence's vision of hearth and home from being, well, *commonplace*, making it both comforting and new. It's a risky gesture, and one designed as much to stabilize a point of departure for subsequent work as it is to gloss the emotional center, or an emotional center, of Finkelstein's project as a whole. As other contributors to this collection point out, Finkelstein's work in other parts of *Scribe*, in *Inside the Ghost Factory*, and in the new, ongoing poems *From the Files of the Immanent Foundation* emphasize strangeness over familiarity—although even in this context it is worth noting that another *Assembly*-era poem, "Tapestry of Light and Dark," insists that we may "hold to the house" even as we "wander in error," our very mistakes and missteps and launchings-outward making us knights errant of some twice-told tale or family romance (*Ratio* 245–46).

Let me close on what will sound, at first, like a mawkishly personal note. There are few poets whose work I love as much as Finkelstein's, and after ten years of straying from poetry and Jewish culture into the study of popular fiction, that affection doesn't seem to have faded. No doubt some of this response stems from my fondness for Norman Finkelstein the person, but I suspect my reaction speaks to something in the work as well. If the British philosopher Simon May is correct that love is what we feel for "those (very rare) people or things or ideas or disciplines or landscapes that can inspire in us a promise of ontological rootedness" (6)—the "hope," as he glosses this phrase, "of an indestructible grounding for our life" (5)—then my love for this work points neither simply to Norman as its author nor simply to something in my background (my having suckled, as Wex says, "at the same cultural bosom," although that's certainly a part of it). Rather, my affective response speaks to aspects of the work itself: the aesthetic and compositional means through which it offers its readers a feeling of at-homeness in its textual world. As we begin to grapple with the gnomic complexity, gnostic aspiration, and gnarly, self-correcting progress of Finkelstein's work, it behooves us to remember how hospitable it is, as well.

Works Cited

Barthes, Roland. *The Pleasure of the Text*. Trans. by Richard Miller. Hill and Wang, 1975.

Boyarin, Daniel. *Border-Lines: The Partition of Judaeo-Christianity*. University of Pennsylvania Press, 2004.

Duncan, Robert. *The Opening of the Field*. Grove Press, 1960.

Finkelstein, Norman. "'The Master of Turning': Walter Benjamin, Gershom Scholem, Harold Bloom, and the Writing of a Jewish Life." In *People of the Book: Thirty Scholars Reflect on Their Jewish Identity*. Jeffrey Rubin-Dorsky and Shelley Fisher Fishkin, eds. University of Wisconsin Press, 1996: 415–426.

———. *The Ratio of Reason to Magic: New and Selected Poems*. Dos Madres Press, 2016.

———. *Restless Messengers*. U of Georgia P, 1992.

———. *Scribe*. Dos Madres Press, 2009.

———. *Track: A Poem*. Shearsman Books, 2012.

Leyb, Mani. "I am ..." Trans. John Hollander. In *The Penguin Book of Modern Yiddish Verse*. Eds. Irving Howe, Ruthe R. Wisse, and Khone Shmeruk. Viking Penguin, 1987: 128–131.

May, Simon. *Love: A History*. Yale University Press, 2011.

Rosten, Leo. *The New Joys of Yiddish*. Three Rivers Press,

Scroggins, Mark. "Woodpaths, Obscure." In *Intricate Thicket: Reading Late Modernist Poetries*. Alabama, 2015: 207–12.

Sedgwick, Eve Kosofsky. *Touching Feeling: Affect, Pedagogy, Performativity*. Duke University Press, 2003.

Selinger, Eric Murphy. "Azoy Toot a Yid: Secular Poetics and 'The Jewish Way." In *Radical Poetics and Secular Jewish Culture*. Stephen Paul Miller and Daniel Morris, eds. University of Alabama Press, 2010: pp. 354–377.

Vendler, Helen. *The Breaking of Style: Hopkins, Heaney, Graham*. Harvard University Press, 1995.

Weinreich, Uriel. *Modern English-Yiddish Yiddish-English Dictionary*. Schocken, 1977.

Wex, Michael. "The Heymish Safari." *New York Jewish Week*, September 6, 2011. http://jewishweek.timesofisrael.com/the heymish-safari/

Yerushalmi, Yosef Haim. *Zakhor: Jewish History and Jewish Memory*. Seattle: University of Washington Press, 1982.

TEXT

No Sympathy for the Devil of History: On "Oppen at Altamont"

Daniel Morris

In " Making The Ghost Walk About Again and Again: History as Séance in the Work of Susan Howe," an essay in *On Mount Vision: Forms of the Sacred in Contemporary American Poetry* (2010), Norman Finkelstein writes, "Functioning as a medium, Howe in effect channels the controversies and debates, the accusations and denials, the spilled blood and spilled ink, and finally, the centuries of chronicles and scholarly research. The poem restages an already highly theatrical chain of events." Finkelstein's comments on Howe as a "medium" resonate with his role in "restag[ing] an already highly theatrical chain of events" connected to the titular subject of "Oppen at Altamont" (2009), among his most visible, and, in my view, most compelling, recent poems. Extending over thirty-nine stanzas, divided into two parts, and running vertically along three distinct columns, the poem first appeared in April 2009 in *Smartish Pace*, and then in *The Ratio of Reason to Magic: New & Selected Poems* (Dos Madres Press, 2016). Jerome Rothenberg also featured "Oppen at Altamont" on his blog in *Jacket* 2 (August 6, 2016). Recalling his reading of Howe, Finkelstein oscillates between subjective, Gnostic, and archival modes in his re-presentation of the audio-visual array of materials that constitute the source texts for "Oppen at Altamont."

Especially in the middle of the three vertical columns, Finkelstein imagines himself as a speaker with a personal stake in the story he is telling (and, to be more precise, to the story of how he has accessed the story he is telling). As the poem's title predicts, the story of the story concerns the peculiar fact that the objectivist poet George Oppen, born in 1908 and so around age 60 at the time, and one of Finkelstein's most enduring influences, joined his wife, Mary, also born in 1908, at the notorious free outdoor rock festival at an obscure Northern California raceway on December 6, 1969. Toiling in a period he describes as characterized by "endless simulacrum," Finkelstein struggles to channel Altamont as historical event while honoring an aesthetic commitment to what Louis Zukofsky, in his introduction to the 1931 "Objectivist" issue of *Poetry*, described as "thinking with the things as they exist." In a literary séance that invokes Oppen as the poet's guiding spirit, Finkelstein nonetheless questions the possibility of recovering the value of his precursor's combination of a Heideggerean epistemology and a poetics devoted to clarity, materiality, limit, ethics, sincerity, and direct witness.

In "Oppen at Altamont," Finkelstein enacts an archival poetics comparable to Howe's, which, as he remarks, combines Gnosticism, lyricism, and historicism. "Oppen at Altamont" also recalls, in form, theme, and sensibility, Oppen's *Of Being Numerous*, which won the 1969 Pulitzer Prize for Poetry. In *Of Being Numerous*, Oppen, prophetically, expresses curiosity about "a new generation" (28, section 26) while exploring themes he and Mary would witness at Altamont to assess their place in a changing world: "There are things / We live among 'and to see them / Is to know ourselves'" (*Of Being Numerous* section 1, page 9). In a raucous environment, Oppen writes, speech fails to ground the self in the world while negotiating differences between persons: "It is not easy to speak // A ferocious mumbling, in public / Of rootless speech" (*OBN* section 17, p. 21). "Of Being Numerous" and "Oppen at Altamont" are assemblages of discrete and yet interrelated pieces of text. In this sense, we may compare both texts in their inchoate affinities to what Finkelstein in his poem refers to as "freeze frames" from *Gimme Shelter*, Albert and David Maysles' 1970 film documentation of the Rolling Stones' 1969 U.S. tour. Recalling a Howe-type séance, which necessitates the poet to "channel" and to "restage" already theatricalized historical material, Finkelstein devotes the right-hand column of "Oppen at Altamont" to generating verbal equivalents—word pictures—to archive, and, implicitly, to enable critical commentary upon, *Gimme Shelter*. Finkelstein reads *Gimme Shelter* as an indelible part of Altamont's situation as an historical event. He coordinates quotations from an Oppen interview about his Altamont experience first published in *Ironwood* and Jagger quotations from *Gimme Shelter* in which the singer engages in futile declarations of communitarianism designed to quell the increasingly violent crowds. He incorporates other quotations from *Gimme Shelter*, including a metafictional scene in which Jagger appears in the filmmaker's editing studio as the Maysles cut their documentary film. Finkelstein also incorporates Oppen's comments about a reading tour he canceled for *Of Being Numerous*, and a bit of conversation between Finkelstein and fellow English professor Alan Golding as they ponder the meaning of Oppen's appearance at the ill-fated concert. As in a Howe literary séance, Finkelstein pulls these fragmentary materials together into a historical recuperation. On a formal level, he evokes the Maysles brothers' *cinema verité* approach to composition as a type of found art. In *Gimme Shelter* and in "Oppen at Altamont," the auteur/poet has based the artifact on the historical record while subjectively rendering the presentness of the past by selectively recomposing disparate audio-visual materials that are "then put together in the cutting room." As Finkelstein stated to me in an email: "I wrote the poem from 2/28/06 to 3/3/06, though I had been planning it and gathering documentary materials for some time before." In *cinema verité*, the director treats frames of film and pieces of sound as distinct material entities that he or she "put[s] together in the cutting room." Just so, Finkelstein's process involved "gathering materials for some time before" he assembled the textual "freeze frames" into a mosaic of three vertical strips.

Critics such as Henry Gould have placed Finkelstein alongside peers such as Peter O'Leary, Joe Donahue, and Ed Foster as key members of a New Gnostic movement in poetry. Finkelstein and the other loose band of authors may chafe against the group designation, but we should recall that *Mount Vision* is part of the title Finkelstein selected for his 2010 study of the place of the spiritual in contemporary poetry. I mention the title to Finkelstein's critical book here because the term *Mount Vision* resembles Altamont. Both place names suggest an elevated space of access to transcendence. In "Oppen at Altamont," however, Oppen's strong suits—materialist objectivism, a concern with the limits to human speech, and the relation of history to representation—chafe against the New Gnostic yearning for sublimity. In "Oppen at Altamont," Finkelstein's mash up of sensibilities ranging from Oppen's to the Maysles Brothers' to Howe's to Allen Ginsberg's to Mick Jagger's traces a chaotic narrative in a form that pivots between rational organization and cacophonous disorientation. Revealing authorial subjectivity, "Oppen at Altamont" criticizes the irresponsibility of an unlimited version of the ecstatic poetics associated with Jagger's dangerously ambitious performativity. He also questions Oppen's ethical culpability as laconic bystander to the Altamont disaster. For Oppen, Altamont signifies the most distressing implications to his concerns about speech as a meaningful form of public communication in an unruly environment, but Finkelstein contemplates the adequacy of Oppen's reserved posture during the distressing concert. "Oppen at Altamont" describes concertgoers as involved in erotic self-satisfaction and yet Finkelstein describes the music as unassigned to any individual voice. At the same time, Finkelstein quotes Oppen as perceiving the "long hair" audience as seeming "to be mourning." One surmises the long hairs are mourning, proactively, a reading such as Finkelstein's own. Interpreting Altamont as a profane version of what René Girard would refer to as ritualized sacred violence, Finkelstein laments how Jagger reigned over a communal Death Drive at the Speedway. Presiding over a mass event that came to "identify death / with a kind of ecstasy / so that the crowd / takes over in a darkness / closely akin to joy," Jagger fancied himself a bardic conjurer in possession of dark knowledge, but "Oppen at Altamont" represents him as a venal fraud. Jagger is most certainly helpless to control the crowd he has whipped into a frenzy once the crush of fans near the small, makeshift stage at the speedway—only a thin cord separated stage from the fans—forced audience members forward, where some accidentally bumped into the Hells Angels' bikes. Described in the poem as "this medieval prince, / troubadour of darkness / self-appointed but / delegated, Jagger tried to pass himself off as a populist by concluding the Stones' U.S. tour with a free West Coast concert. Finkelstein, by contrast, perceives Jagger as a greedy aristocrat. On his American tour in 1969, as Joel Selvin has noted, Jagger wanted to establish his street cred at a point in rock history when the genre was tilting away from the English Invasion and in the direction of bands developing in the Bay Area (*Santana, The Grateful Dead, Jefferson Airplane* and Janis Joplin among them). Cynically, Jagger sought to benefit from the free outdoor event at Altamont by profiting from *Gimme Shelter's* ticket receipts. Jagger confused the corporate Death Drive with a desire for the erasure of self and the extinction of the discerning sensibility responsible for the consequences of language. Such discernment characterizes the reticent sensibility Finkelstein's speaker as he channels Oppen's legacy. Jagger never took responsibility for the bloody aftermath to his oracular pretense. *Gimme Shelter* and "Oppen at Altamont" also document how festival staff escorted Jagger off the stage and to safety in San Francisco via helicopter. By contrast, Meredith Hunter, a fan in the first row repeatedly stabbed by Hells Angels member Al Passaro, bled to death because no helicopters were available to shuttle him to a Bay Area trauma center. A communal instance of the repetition compulsion of traumatic events at Vietnam and at Altamont, Finkelstein interprets the helicopter in his poem as at once reminding us and shielding us from the terror of "the fall of Saigon / reenacted endlessly / in a musical."

In the essay on Howe from *Mount Vision*—the phrase *Mount Vision* appears in Howe's poem "Thorow" (1990)—Finkelstein offers a salutary, if still paradoxical, way to understand a visionary poetics as in the service of recuperating historical understanding:

> In Howe's work, the visual and aural elements are equally important, which is why "You're hearing something you see." Indeed, the strangely "unreadable" print collages found in most of her poems could be viewed as materializations of dead voices, both from old books and historical personages, which partially reveal themselves through the "medium" of the text. Her reference to her "hand receiving orders from somewhere" also points to the poem as séance: spirit writing, taking written dictation from spirits guiding one's pen, was

a specialty of many mediums and a favored mode of communication with the dead.

In his Howe essay, and, by extension, in "Oppen at Altamont," Finkelstein explores the contradictory mixture of violence, representation, history, and memory that he associates with René Girard's theory of violence and the sacred: "Indeed, the sacred may be understood as containing within itself the notion of blasphemy or transgression. At such moments—and they are ubiquitous in Howe's work—the poet approaches what Girard calls 'the two faces of the sacred—the interplay of order and disorder, of difference lost and retrieved'" (*Violence* 257). An archival pastiche as well as coherent spatial display with the three vertical columns divided in two sections, "Oppen at Altamont" most certainly exhibits Girard's "interplay of order and disorder, of difference lost and retrieved." In the left hand column of the poem, Finkelstein focuses on themes of "mourning," prophecy, and the contested relationships among generations in a crowd that is "always at risk/as power in unleashed." This last theme seems inevitable. Mary and George were forty years older than most who attended Altamont. On a historical level, the left hand column's description of a "spike" that, the poet says, can lead to a knife, refers to Pesaro's weapon. On the level of visionary poetry, Finkelstein is referencing Genesis 22, the Akedah, or the binding of Isaac. Translating Altamont as the High Mount, we may link the concert location to the biblical situation at Mount Moriah. However obliquely, Finkelstein has joined historical and visionary modes in a fashion reminiscent of his critical treatment of Susan Howe. He reads Hunter's murder at Altamont as a perverse Midrash on Genesis 22. In opposition to Genesis 22, however, in which the Angel's voice calls Abraham to halt his murderous intent, it is the Hells Angel, Passaro, who murders Hunter, an innocent member of the younger generation.

In his representation of Oppen in the left-hand column, Finkelstein casts the objectivist poet as a "meditative man." Oppen, the poem declares, was able to "honorably keep / His distance" from Altamont's mayhem. Oppen certainly avoided Jagger's irresponsible solipsism, and yet one senses Finkelstein considers Oppen's circumspection and detachment as themselves signs of impotence in the face of a public crisis.

But to what degree

> does one withdraw from the stage?
> Oppen cancels his reading tour—
> "woke up one night in the absolute certainty
> that I could not do it…
> cannot, cannot, perhaps particularly
> with the expansion of voice in Numerous
> I cannot make a Chautauqua of it,
> cannot put myself so thoroughly INTO it,
> like a Ginsberg."

Finkelstein implicates Oppen in Altamont's catastrophe if only because the objectivist poet's diffidence about overstepping his bounds as a speaker on behalf of other minds discouraged the beloved precursor from participating in "a Chautauqua," Oppen's surprisingly derogatory term for an outdoor cultural event that features audience engagement in a carnivalesque atmosphere. In an email to me, Finkelstein described the middle column as reflecting the view of "the poet." There are, however, quotations that appear in the left hand column—that is, the column Finkelstein devoted to the Rolling Stones—that reference Oppen's published views. Oppen and Jagger primarily appear in opposite columns in Finkelstein's poem, but "Oppen at Altamont" is concerned with generational affiliation as much as it is with generational conflict and so the lines between Oppen and Jagger blur into one another from time to time. The poem's middle column, which Finkelstein refers to as "the poet" column, refers to Finkelstein, but also to Oppen and to Ginsberg. *Contra* Oppen, Ginsberg represents an embrace of the "Chautauqua" style of interaction between singer and audience that Finkelstein reads as foreshadowing Jagger's tragic misinterpretation of the Hells Angels as benign participants in a collective celebration of music, youthful experimentation, and freedom from the restraints of conventional behavior:

> Who once invited
> the Angels to
> a Dylan concert, calling
> them "our outlaw
> brothers of the
> counterculture"

In the middle column, the poet repudiates Ginsberg's legacy by casting the Beat icon's impulsive poetics as predicting the naïve, deluded, and hubristic behavior of a Jagger. Jagger and Ginsberg, however, are not the only singers that Finkelstein associates with "unleashing/energies" through expansive song. The phrase "unleashing/energies" resonates with Oppen's concern that the "expansion of voice in ["On Being] *Numerous*" replicates the unauthorized voice of the "people" or "crowd" that Finkelstein, in the middle column of "Oppen at Altamont," associates with unregulated violence. In an email to me, Finkelstein said he is "responding most centrally" to section 10 of *Of Being Numerous*:

> Or, in that light, New arts! Dithyrambic, audience-as-artists! But I will listen to a man, I will listen to a man, and when I speak I will speak, tho he will fail and I will fail. But I will listen to him speak. The shuffling of a crowd is nothing—well, nothing but the many that we are, but nothing.
> Urban art, art of the cities, art of the young in the cities—The isolated man is dead, his world around his exhausted
> And he fails! He fails, that meditative man! And indeed they can not 'bear' it. (section 10, p. 15)

Alluding to a passage in "Of Being Numerous" that follows Oppen's powerful line about "the bright light of shipwreck," and that appears in a section associating "that light" with the "Dithyrambic," we realize that Finkelstein is correlating Oppen's poetics and Jagger's theatrics at Altamont with rhythmic performance in ancient Greek Dionysian ritual festivals. Finkelstein himself rehearses Ginsberg's oracular, anaphoric, and dithyrambic type of rhetoric in his poem, but this festive style describes Jagger's inability to distinguish persons representing real and present dangers from a dandified, androgynous, and theatrical fantasy of Satanic Dionysian revelry: "Who once invited the Angels to a Dylan concert, calling them 'our outlaw brothers of the counterculture.'" Focusing on Whitman's penchant for self-celebration rather than on Whitman's coincidental interest in representing the crowd with a formal approach to managing lines and strophes that distinguishes between part and whole, Finkelstein casts Jagger's performance at Altamont as creating a paradoxically "masturbatory atmosphere" that doubles as an impersonal love fest in which "the songs … are no one's own." Jagger can, unconvincingly, and with a tragic lack of success, urge the unruly crowd to "show/we're all one," but that only leads to the problem that "The Crowd" is "always at risk" as "power is unleashed." As Burt Hatlen has written, Oppen, too, was concerned with "the ontology of the human collectivity" and the "ongoing life of the people 'en masse.'" Oppen writes in "On Being Numerous": "We want to say // 'common sense' / And cannot" (part 26) and, in part nine, Oppen writes, "Whether, as intensity of seeing increases, one's distance from Them, the people, does not also increase." Oppen is attracted to and repelled by "The absolute singular," which is "the bright light of shipwreck." He and Mary attended Altamont, but "Oppen at Altamont" describes them as seeming "odd" "to any of the festive youth/unstoned and thoughtful." Like Oppen before him, Finkelstein seeks accuracy in representation through documentary methods while acknowledging the inevitable role mediation plays in distorting our recollection of the past. "Oppen at Altamont" suggests the limits of representation in that "neither the Maysles nor mine/can present this passage," this "sickening acceleration/that no poem may stop."

Like Oppen before him, Finkelstein occupies a circumspect posture. He approaches writing with a pronounced concern for the ethics of speaking on behalf of others when the outcomes to his utterance may conceal truth, blur distinctions between discrete entities, or encourage violence. Like Ginsberg before him, Jagger, by contrast to Oppen, signifies in Finkelstein's poem the cultic singer. At Altamont, Jagger seems woefully unprepared to deal with the aftermath to his Bacchanalian performance. He failed to assess the outcomes to his speech acts or to take responsibility for performing in a manner that contributed to an atmosphere that encouraged irrational behavior. Self-scrutiny was not Jagger's strong suit. The middle column of "Oppen at Altamont," by contrast, is devoted to Oppen's ambivalence about the efficacy, outcomes, and questionable legitimacy of the poet who elects, on his own authority, to speak on behalf of a group. Oppen's poetry conveys to readers the sense that silence may well be preferable to speech in certain situations. As with the physicians' Hippocratic Oath, Finkelstein recommends that at least the poet do no harm. When describing his and Mary's experience at Altamont, Oppen's focus is on describing with fidelity the physical scene itself: "the irrigation canals" and "walking under the high-tension wires over the brown hills". "Unstoned" and "thoughtful," Oppen uses language to establish a material world outside the self. The goal is to dispute nihilism. Oppen's limited poetics contradicts Jagger's use of language to promote a romanticized assessment of simulacrum.

The middle column of "Oppen at Altamont" emphasizes the poet's ambivalent, even contradictory, and, at times, bitter, relation to speech. Speech acts, the poet states in the middle column, range from "corrupted" to essential components of a functioning polis: "we are able to live/only because some things have been said." Speech contributes to the "corruption" Finkelstein refers to "endless simulacrum," which he associates with *Gimme Shelter*, a representation indelibly intertwined with our memory of the murderous incidents at Altamont. Oppen and Finkelstein seek to distinguish corrupt speech from speech that promotes communication between persons, but in part two of the middle column, Finkelstein abandons hope that he can recover Oppen's Heideggerian claims that speech can push through falsehood to enable us "to live." Each of the three short stanzas in part two casts a Platonic pall over Finkelstein's recovery of Dasein. Instead of being, Finkelstein seeks stillness. In part two of the middle column, one could say the poet, paradoxically, prefers the stasis of photography to the temporal conditions of writing, or film for that matter. This is so even as the poet wishes to situate representation and reality in a proximate relationship that provides a counterweight to "endless simulacrum." In "Oppen at Altamont," Finkelstein associates "endless simulacrum" with the oscillation between Altamont the concert as actual event and Altamont as it appears in *Gimme Shelter*, as well as with the specific image of the helicopter, which played a key role in Altamont, the contemporaneous Vietnam War, and, more recently, the Broadway musical *Miss Saigon*. To my surprise, the elegiac tone of part two of the middle column reminded me of Wallace Stevens' very late poems. In "This Solitude of Cataracts" (1954), for example, Stevens's speaker admits, "He never felt twice the same about the flecked river, / Which kept flowing and never the same way twice." At the risk of courting death as a form of stasis, "He wanted to feel the same way over and over" and to "walk beside" a river "flowing the same way" and "beneath a moon nailed fast" in "a permanent realization" (*Collected Poems* 449). At the end of the middle section of "Oppen at Altamont," the poet stands helpless, like Walter Benjamin's Janus-faced Angel of History, as he surveys his contribution to an endlessly repetitive loop of tragedy and defeat. At the same time, he acknowledges that no poem, no representation, may stop time or alter what happened at Altamont. Drafting "Oppen at Altamont" at age sixty—comparable to Oppen's age in 1969—Finkelstein must have experienced the chill of time's swift passage. And yet the two stanzas preceding the concluding one represent an "endless simulacra." In the third to last stanza, history becomes frozen, as in a broken film loop, at the moment the Stones escape the deadly havoc at Altamont via helicopter.

Finkelstein's has described the right-hand column of the poem as devoted to Jagger and the Rolling Stones. He does name Jagger and Charlie Watts, the band's drummer, in the right-hand column, but I would describe this column as repeating in words what Finkelstein twice in the same column refers to as "freeze frame" images of Altamont from *Gimme Shelter*. The verbal equivalents of film stills range from depicting Jagger "helpless onstage" as he shouts platitudes of unity to the unruly crowd, to Charlie Watts, the Stones' drummer, staring "in reverie" at a mosaic scene reminiscent of a "biblical painting" in which the Hells Angels clear a "path to the stage" for the performers "as the bikes roar through." In a disillusioned metacommentary on the

95

outcome to his ekphrasis, Finkelstein, in part two of the right hand column, admits his repetition of prior representations about Altamont has failed to provide the reader with a relation to the event that might promote a cathartic working through of trauma. The poet acknowledges his representation to be one more sounding in an echo chamber that veils, rather than reveals, history, but such an analysis cannot alter a baseline fact: a discredited maker, Jagger, "stares at us forever." It is not Oppen's ethical poetics that remains visible at the end of the poem, but the face of the thoroughly commercialized singer who failed to read his audience while "No arbitrary free-frame / neither the Maysles nor mine / can prevent this passage."

In "Reticence and Rhetorics: The Poetry of George Oppen," Michael André Bernstein emphasizes Oppen's treatment of his writing as "a store-house of gathering from different domains of experience," but also as revealing, "an equally strong sense of the limitations in any one man's mind or language, limitations that severely restrict how much of that larger world he can honestly (again, the unavoidable word) grasp" (234–5). In "Of Being Numerous," Oppen expresses uncertainty about the outcomes to his speech acts. He is especially concerned with the difficult, if not impossible, goal of writing a type of meditative poetry that succeeds as few poems have done in negotiating the relationship between speaker and audience without falling into nihilism or unauthorized speech on behalf of other persons who can do just fine speaking for themselves. Finkelstein's "Oppen at Altamont" honors his precursor's willingness to document a reality beyond the self while acknowledging the limitations of speech as a way to put a halt to violence, to uncover the thoughts of other minds, to alleviate trauma, or to enable readers to achieve a sense, after Heidegger, of ever Being There.

Works Cited

Bernstein, Michael André. "Reticence and Rhetorics: The Poetry of George Oppen." Ed. Burton Hatlen. *George Oppen: Man and Poet*. Orono, Maine:

The National Poetry Foundation, 1981. 231–238.

Finkelstein, Norman. "Making The Ghost Walk About Again and Again: History as Séance in the Work of Susan Howe. *On Mount Vision: Forms of the Sacred in Contemporary American Poetry.* Iowa City: University of Iowa Press, 2010.

———. *The Ratio of Reason to Magic: New & Selected Poems.* Loveland, Ohio: Madres Press, 2016.

Gould, Henry. "'I gather the limbs of Osiris': Notes on the New Gnosticism." *Coldfront.* May 9, 2014. http:/coldfrontmag.com/i-gather the limbs-of-osiris-noted-on-the-new-gnosticism/

O'Leary, Peter. "The Energies of Words." Poetry Foundation website. https://www.poetryfoundation.org/articles/69068/the-energies-of-words Originally published June 12, 2008.

Oppen, George. *Of Being Numerous.* New York: New Directions Press, 1967.

Perloff, Marjorie. The Shipwreck of the Singular: George Oppen's "Of Being Numerous." http://bigbridge.org/BB14/PerloffShipwreck.pdf

Selvin, Joel. *Altamont: The Rolling Stones, The Hell Angels, and the Inside Story of Rock's Darkest Day.* New York: Harper Collings, 2016.

Stevens, Wallace. "The Solitude of Cataracts." *The Collected Poems of Wallace Stevens.* New York: Vintage, 2015. 449.

White, Dave. "Woodstock 101: Four days that changed the world." March 17, 2017. ThoughtCo. https://www.thoughtco.com/history-of-woodstock-748354

Lyric of Disaster / Disaster of Lyric: On Norman Finkelstein's *Track*

Henry Weinfield

"*Track* is the lyric of disaster, the disaster of lyric," Norman Finkelstein writes in the "Statements for *Track*" he collected for the Shearsman Books edition of the poem that appeared in 2012 (303). This assertion is clarified by the poem's title, much as the title is clarified by the assertion; for if, among many other possibilities, the track of the poem's title leads ineluctably to the death camps, then the assertion partly alludes to Adorno's famous pronouncement of 1949 that "to write poetry after Auschwitz is barbaric." Adorno did not actually specify *lyric* poetry, but his pronouncement is often quoted as if he had, perhaps because he was associating poetry with the "lyrical" values of beauty and refinement, and asserting that continuing to pursue such values as if nothing had happened was barbaric. And if, for Adorno, the disaster of the Shoah ruptured the fabric of civilized life, putting all humanistic values and ideals into question, including traditional aesthetic ones, then it would also, in Finkelstein's phrase, have constituted the disaster of lyric—especially if the lyric is construed (as it all too often is by American poets and critics) as an unmediated expression of the self. As Adorno was himself aware, however, his pronouncement was markedly one-sided. In his great essay of 1957, "On Lyric Poetry and Society," he writes: "The universality of the lyric's substance ... is social in nature. Only one who hears the voice of humankind in the poem's solitude can understand what the poem is saying" (1:38). Here, Auschwitz does not enter into the equation because lyric is being conceived not as an exercise in narcissism but as "the voice of humankind"; it is only if the lyric is viewed as an unmediated expression of the self that the problem of "bad faith" becomes relevant. In recent years, the Language Poets have taken a sledgehammer to lyric subjectivity, to the ubiquitous "lyric poetry" of creative writing workshops. Their critique is understandable and to a certain extent salutary, but the question is whether in substituting "language" (i.e. some sort of autonomous process) for a debased conception of lyric subjectivity they are not simply reenacting the *enantiodromia* (Jung's term for the violent oscillation between opposed principles or positions) that is characteristic of American poetry generally.

There is, of course, a middle ground between the Language Poets and the various confessional tendencies that remain dominant in contemporary American poetry. It was articulated by Mallarmé in his great essay *Crise de vers* (1886) when he wrote: "The pure work [of poetry] implies the disappearance of the poet as speaker, who cedes the initiative to the words themselves..." (my translation; 366). The impact of Mallarmé on the avant-garde, especially on its American adherents, has come mainly through his revolutionary free-verse poem of 1897, *Un coup de dés* (which, as it happens, is among other things a confrontation with disaster), but Mallarmé was above all a lyric poet in the classical sense, and in the statement from *Crise de vers* he takes it for granted that ceding the initiative to the words themselves is made possible by verse—that is, by the exigencies of meter and rhyme.

Be this as it may, the "disaster of lyric" to which Finkelstein refers is multi-determined. One of its tracks—and hence one of the tracks leading to *Track*—is history, considered as a series of disasters. But there is also the history of poetry to consider. Beginning in the eighteenth century, prose swallows up all of the other poetic genres until, by a certain point, only the lyric remains; but then, with the advent of modernism, lyric poetry begins to undergo and enact a series of crises of its own. The movement toward free verse coincides with a tendency toward fragmentation, not only because after World War 1 the culture is increasingly perceived as being in ruins, but, in the absence of meter and rhyme, because poetry needs to distinguish itself from prose in order to ensure its continued existence and pursue its course as poetry. This is a Faustian bargain, however, for while the reliance on fragmentation allows gifted poets to achieve a certain kind of ghostly lyricism—a "lyric of disaster," in Finkelstein's phrase—it further narrows the scope of poetry and takes its revenge in various other ways.

Paradoxically, it is from the standpoint of fragmentation and of the fragment, of a lyric of disaster that confronts not only disaster in general but the disaster of lyric as well, that Finkelstein attempts to construct a long poem—and indeed, in the single-volume Shearsman edition, *Track* stretches to more than three hundred pages. The poem is unified—insofar as a poem that confronts ruin and the impossibility of unity can be unified—by two factors: first, by the sense of loss with which it is pervaded and which makes it, from beginning to end, one long elegy, and, second, by the various "recombinatory" procedures through which its material is largely generated. As Nathaniel Mackey writes on the back cover of the Shearsman edition, *Track* "undertakes a voyage beset by recombinatory duress." Mackey's point is that Finkelstein's material is generated partly by puns, rhymes, and other figures that keep combining in a variety of ways. The figures are continually refigured, the combinations recombined, and thus the process may be said to be "recombinatory." But what is truly fundamental to Finkelstein's project, giving the poetry of *Track* its peculiar texture and the ghostly lyricism it is sometimes able to achieve, is that the sense of sadness and loss pervading the poem is not linked to any *specific* events or disasters, or indeed to anything in particular. Thus, while Finkelstein's project is certainly inflected by Language Poetry, there is a sense in which it hearkens back to the methods of the Symbolists.

One of my favorite moments in *Track* occurs in the first of the poem's three sections, *Forest*. This moment (or poem, or lyric, or fragment) strikes me as typical of what Finkelstein is saying and doing, and also of what he is able to achieve in this mode:

> Founder or finder
> you among the many
> traced to the city
> you among the lost

> You among the last
> voices from Paradise
> founder founder
> whispers the finder. (62)

What do we make of these lines? It might seem that I have taken them out of context, but in fact there is none: the poem offers us scarcely any contextual markers, and in effect we are on our own. There is a city, perhaps an ancient one, but we aren't told; perhaps it was *founded* by some mythical or legendary figure, but he, like all the other inhabitants, is now lost. The "finder," who may or may not belong to a later time than the "founder," is himself "among the many / traced to the city," but in some unspecified way: it may be that he came upon or *found* the city in a physical sense, just as the "founder" *founded* it, but he could also be a scholar who is studying it; in any event, he too is, or will be, "among the lost." It is clear that, from a linguistic point of view, the "founder" and "finder" are generated by each other—that is, by a purely linguistic procedure tantamount to rhyme—and the same can be said about the connection that is then drawn between the words "lost" and "last," a connection that generates the second quatrain. The parallel that leaps across the quatrains between "you among the lost" and "You among the last" is eloquently expressed, but it is immediately undercut by the irony of enjambment, as a result of which "last," in addition to modifying the unmentioned people of the city, also modifies the "voices from Paradise" of the next line. What voices from Paradise? We aren't told, but the implication is that the lost city is being connected to Paradise, perhaps because we tend to conceive of the past nostalgically as a paradise.

In the first six lines, there is no speaker other than the poet or lyric-I, but the last two lines of the poem are *whispered* by the "finder." Is this "finder" the same as the one in the opening quatrain or is he the poet himself? Has the "finder" (of the city? or of the founder?) stepped beyond the threshold of his own time and merged with the poet, who, in his invention or discovery, has become a "finder" in his own right, or has the poet stepped into the time-frame of his contemplation? And finally, is the "finder" at the end of the second quatrain invoking the "founder" in the quatrain's penultimate line, or is "founder" in that line a verb? The absence of punctuation would seem to indicate that the ambiguity is deliberate and that both interpretations are valid. If so, the "finder," whoever he may be, is invoking the "founder," but also reflecting on the fact that all things *founder*, fall into ruin or disaster.

As I noted, the terms "founder" and "finder," "lost" and "last," are generated linguistically by one another. But what is crucial is that in this case they are also generated *thematically*. These symbolic concepts are part of a poetic constellation which, though it is not linked to anything specific in the world, is poetically meaningful in and of itself. (This is what makes the poem's technique akin to that employed by the French Symbolists.) The poem is not referential, but it is also not cut off from meaning. It would be a mistake to consider it vague, for its intention is not to refer to anything in particular but rather to arrive at a clarity and precision of another kind—and this its rhythm forcefully conveys. This is genuine poetry.

In our correspondence on the *Track* project, which occurred over the course of a number of years, I mentioned to Finkelstein that I wished he had put more of his own immediate experience into the poem, and he alludes to this in his "Statements" (305). Let me take the opportunity to say that I now think this criticism was completely wrong-headed. Insofar as the poem has weaknesses, they have nothing to do with the lack of contextual markers or with the lyric distance the poet establishes. The problem is rather that the moments of lyric intensity, such as the "Founder or finder" passage I have just discussed, are interspersed with weaker passages in which the poet's inspiration flags. The fault has to do with the American ambition (an ambition amounting almost to a mania) to attempt a long poem when neither the conceptual nor the technical basis for one really exists. Under the aegis of American capitalist print culture—and I think this tendency has only been exacerbated by the advent of the Internet—the unit of value has long been the book rather than the individual poem (as it should be), and so poets have been under an unnatural compunction to think in terms of books and to write more and more—when more is obviously less where poetry is concerned. So, I wish that Finkelstein had conceived of *Track* not as a single poem but rather as a sequence of lyrics, in which case it might then have been easier for him to weed away the lesser material. As the poem now stands, it accumulates but does not really develop. Its gestures are endlessly repeated, and between the extraordinary moments there is a fair amount of stasis and marking time.

As I have suggested, in order for the "recombinatory" procedures to be persuasive, they have to be mirrored by a conception (what Emerson called a "metre-making argument); they cannot simply give rise to an arbitrary one; language and theme must be mutually generative for poetry of this kind (or indeed any kind) to be successful. This does not always happen, however. The following variations from *Columns*, the second section of the poem, provide an example of the problem implicit in the poem's method:

> Why acquiesce
> to all that is demanded?
>
> Why demand
> that all acquiesce?
>
> #
>
> It is a history
> of demands and acquiescence
>
> A history of repetitions
> which constitute a life.

The sense of fatalism conveyed by the initial question, and also by the last four lines, is certainly genuine; but the second question ("Why demand / that all acquiesce?") seems generated merely by the technique of reversal. Granted that the question makes sense, but the problem it poses is not one that the poet happens to be grappling with: *he* is not the one who would be making such a demand, in any event, and so the question seems gratuitous. If the issue of sincerity arises, it has nothing to do with the "experiencing subject," which is an extraneous concern, but rather with the artistic process, with the poet's shaping of his material. Of course, if poetry is nothing more than a "recombinatory" game, then the issue of artistic sincerity is irrelevant; in that case, however, poetry itself, as an art form, is itself irrelevant.

Courageous as it is, *Track* is a product of its time—as all poems of course are. Inflected (and, to a certain extent, infected) by the formalistic procedures of Language Poetry, it fails to distinguish— even to itself—when it has something important to say and when it doesn't, when it is on the right track and when it has gone off the rails; and so brilliant passages often lie cheek by jowl with duller ones. It has many of the faults of the contemporary avant-garde: it is too self-regarding and mannered, and, because poets nowadays "lead their lives / Among poets" (despite George Oppen's admonition), it is sometimes pitched to too narrow and easily satisfied an audience. Nevertheless, it possesses a philosophical intelligence and a largeness of scope that are exceedingly rare. And most importantly, it contains passages of great beauty, passages in which the attempt to confront the "disaster of lyric" through a "lyric of disaster" offers us a momentary glimpse of transcendence.

Works Cited:

Adorno, Theodor W. "On Lyric Poetry and Society." Notes to Literature. Trans. Shierry Weber Nicholson. New York: Columbia UP, 1991. 2 vols.

Finkelstein, Norman. *Track*. Bristol, UK: Shearsman Books, 2012.

Mallarmé, Stéphane, *Œuvres complètes*. Ed. Henri Mondor and G. Jean-Aubry. Paris: Gallimard, 1945.

Thaumaturgical energy pulses through the corridors: Gnostic transmission in Norman Finkelstein's *From the Files of the Immanent Foundation*

Peter O'Leary

Antoine Faivre, the great scholar of Hermeticism, insists that Gnosis "is a sacred, saving philosophy, soteriological because it effects the inner transformation of man, not through discursive thought but according to [Henry] Corbin [the legendary scholar of Islamic mysticism], through a narrative revelation of hidden things, a saving light that itself brings life and joy, a divine grace that operates and assures salvation."[1] Sometime in the early teens, Norman Finkelstein began to write the poems in his late book-length sequence *From the Files of the Immanent Foundation.* Finkelstein describes the poems in this sequence as constituting a "hidden narrative," one in which deflections, obfuscations, surreality, and something of the monotony of memoranda enable "certain effects commonly associated with narrative." Commenting on the Foundation itself, he claims, "it is not a governmental agency, not a sect or cult, not a fraternal organization, not a think tank, not a research institution—but I think it 'exists' in the spaces between and behind all such entities. It is unquestionably hermetic, and the search for gnosis plays an important part in its self-definition and activities."[2] "Appointment," a poem early <u>in the sequence,</u> begins:

1. Antoine Faivre, "Esotericism," in Hidden Truths: Magic, Alchemy, and the Occult, ed. Lawrence E. Sullivan (New York: Macmillan, 1989), 40.
2. Norman Finkelstein, *The Ratio of Reason to Magic* (Loveland, OH: Dos Madres Press, 2016), 359.

> So the trout really was her grandfather,
> and everybody around there were cousins,
> more or less. It appears to be the realm
> of freedom, but there are still constraints.
> The facades suggest otherwise, and beyond them,
> rooms opening upon rooms, infinite hallways,
> dreams of a mansion made of nooks and corners,
> window seats to look down upon kitchen
> gardens, the meadows and hills beyond.
> The Directors have gone to considerable trouble
> to arrange all this.[3]

The straightforward if wryly and bureaucratically obscure language and phrasing of this selection is typical of the whole sequence. Finkelstein comments that the order of the poems as they appear in the selection in *The Ratio of Reason to Magic* is not the order in which they were written, "[u]nlike much of my other work," he claims. To this he adds, "[P]art of my efforts have involved arranging them to produce certain effects commonly associated with narrative."[4] To repeat lines from "Appointment," *The Directors have gone to considerable trouble / to arrange all this.* It appears to be true that they have. Mythos in Aristotle's definition, made famous to Black Mountaineers by Jane Harrison by way of Robert Duncan, *is the arrangement of the incidents.* In *Themis,* her extensive meditation on the social origins of Greek religion, Harrison asserts that the primary sense of *mythos* is "simply the thing uttered," elaborating:

> From sounds made by the mouth, to words spoken and thence to tale
> or story told the transition is easy. Always there is the same antithesis
> of speech and action which are but two different ways of expressing
> emotion, two forms of reaction; the *mythos,* the tale told, the action
> recounted, is contrasted with the action actually done. It is from this
> antithesis that the sense of unreality, non-existence gradually arises.[5]

3. Norman Finkelstein, *From the Files of the Immanent Foundation* (Loveland, OH: Dos Madres, 2018), 6.
4. Finkelstein, *New & Selected Poems,* 359.
5. Jane Ellen Harrison, *Themis* (London: Merlin Press, 1963), 328.

Robert Duncan refers to this as "the principle of life," arising from the ideal poetic quest for both "meaningful life and dread *psychosis*" at once.[6] Kafka presupposes the mythical sense of unreality gradually arising that augurs Finkelstein's Foundation when he writes, "If what was supposed to be destroyed in Paradise was destructible, then it can't have been decisive; however, if it was indestructible, then we are living in a false belief."[7] Finkelstein's Foundation, whose directors have gone to considerable trouble to arrange things for us, coordinates meaningful life and unreliable paradise, psychosis and dream, freedom and constraint.

The effect of the poems in *From the Files of the Immanent Foundation* is tidal—the reader is sucked back in to an oceanic feeling, a sense of looming, shadowy drowning, in which flashes of language serve as life preservers. Are these poems of a bureaucratic Gnosticism, contrary to Faivre's claims, anti-soteriological? Not quite. Rather, they go against the grain of salvation but not antagonistically. Instead, they roughen the texture of the Gnosis they uncover while also smoothing the edges. It's no secret that these poems emerged during the period of Finkelstein's training in psychoanalysis to become a lay analyst. These are poems of magic and crisis, mystery and confidence together.

"Narrative" is the operative term in Finkelstein's characterization of this work. The word is crucially found as well in Faivre's description of esoteric Gnosis, which manifests "through a narrative of hidden things," availed in an act of "interiorism," which Faivre describes as "an entry into the self through a special knowledge or gnosis, in order to attain a form of enlightenment or individual salvation. This special knowledge concerns the relationships that unite us to God or to the divine world.... To learn these relationships, the individual must enter, or 'descend,' into himself by means of an initiatory process, progressing along a path that is hierarchically structured by a series of intermediaries."[8] In effect, these relationships become known—their

6. Robert Duncan, *Collected Essays and Other Prose*, edited by James Maynard (Berkeley: University of California Press, 2014), 140.
7. Franz Kafka, *The Zürau Aphorisms*, number 74, translated by Michael Hofmann (New York: Schocken Books, 2006), 73.
8. Faivre, 38–9.

meaning revealed—not through epiphany but through a journey. In the case of the Immanent Foundation, this is a journey configured as a visit to a vast yet personal, daunting yet peculiar office building where the people are friendly but inscrutable. This, you ask somewhat incredulously, is Finkelstein's vision of esoteric Gnosis? Yes it is, and think about it. What is more hierarchical than a bureaucracy? And who better to serve as intermediaries in such a hierarchy than office workers?

"Executive" begins like this:

> Lucy hands in a message inscribed upon a shard.
> It is time to go. Birch wand or willow wand?
> The dowser will tell us. And a lantern, for the way
> is dark. But look here. On the surface of the glass,
> a pleat, and in the glass, a troupe of dancers,
> bound together by a single thread.
> Later, the speaker of the poem extemporizes:
> Look around. The inscription
> on the wall of the library, the—yes, yes—the
> scriptorium, completes the one at hand.
> Three hands, an eye, a hawk, a shod foot,
> a dagger, an eye, an ibis. You say this distresses you,
> that it troubles your heart?[9]

Is the Executive the one who is speaking in the poem? And who is Lucy? She's an intermediary, of course, just as the Executive sits atop an esoteric hierarchy. The diction of these lines, and their associations, provide the sense the Immanent Foundation poems activate: The opening lines suggest young-adult fantasy literature, blended just slightly with a choose-your-own-adventure format: "Birch wand or willow wand?" The opening suggestions of young adult literature yield to something more institutionally bound but inscrutably so. There's a library, there are inscriptions, there is even a monastic scriptorium (without any evidence of monks or scribes), and then there are crypto-magical items presented in a list: three hands, an eye, a hawk, a shod foot, a dagger, an eye, and an ibis. Items for a divination? Some kind of

9. Finkelstein, *Immanent Foundation*, 11.

tarot? The ibis is a traditional symbol for Thoth, the ancient Egyptian god, lord of Hermopolis and scribe of the gods. He is identified with Hermes and, by extension, assimilated to Hermes Trismegistus, the legendary Thrice-greatest magician and sage of Alexandria, also known as Thoth-Hermes the "hypomnemotographer," or secretary to the gods.[10] If something is distressing us, it may perhaps be the insouciant ease with which the speaker of the poem—and by extension Finkelstein himself, drifts through these mytho-historical suggestions, peripherally hypnotizing us as we wander through the corridors of the foundation. The phrasing in this particular poem proceeds by way of a tone of gentle but disturbing instruction, characterized by the phrase, "But look here," a tone that persists throughout these poem. When you pause to look, the details leave you queasy. Not just because they are surreal. Rather, because they evince the surplus of dream.

In his note about the selection from the sequence that appears in his selected poems, *The Ratio of Reason to Magic*, Finkelstein indicates that the Foundation "seems to be in a state of crisis," a state in which it might always already be.[11] Finkelstein connects this state to the condition of "Egyptomania" identified by Eric Santner in his book *The Psychotheology of Everyday Life*, which Santner characterizes as a fantasy of absorptive restraint in the Jewish imagination (think of Freud's brilliant *Moses and Monotheism* as a kind of Egyptomania) from which—through the fantasies of which—some form of exodus is possible. In effect, we wander the labyrinthine corridors and scenes of the Immanent Foundation in order to escape from it.

We should examine this Egyptomania, such as it is, further. Santner identifies in it a "too muchness," an "uncanny vitality" pressuring up from the unconscious:

> We are, in a crucial sense, placed in the space of relationality not by
> way of intentional acts but rather by a kind of *unconscious transmission*
> that is neither simply enlivening nor simply deadening but rather, if
> I might put it that way, *undeadening*; it produces in us an internal

---

10. See Antoine Faivre, *The Eternal Hermes: From Greek God to Alchemical Magus*, translated by Jocelyn Godwin (Grand Rapids, MI: Phanes Press, 1995), pp. 76-80.
11. Finkelstein, *New and Selected Poems*, 359.

alienness that has a peculiar sort of vitality and yet *belongs to no form of life*. What I am calling "undeadness" is thus correlative to the encounter—above all in the life of a child—with the Other's desire and the seemingly endless drama of legitimation it inaugurates.[12]

This "surplus excitation," whose expression consists of repeated "enigmatic messages" that constitute the "event of revelation" is itself, richly, a mysterious encounter with that great vitality belonging to no form of life, the unconscious, which Santner characterizes by way of Kafka as "the fundamental place of fantasy." "To put it paradoxically," he clarifies, "what matters most in a human life may in some sense be one's specific form of *disorientation*, the idiomatic way in which one's approach to and movement through the world is 'distorted.'"[13]

Disorientation. Distortion. In other words, the sacred, the holy. Rudolf Otto calls holiness "a category of interpretation and valuation peculiar to the sphere of religion," adding "that it completely eludes apprehension in terms of concepts."[14] Otto makes clear that while the category of the Holy includes great moral resonance, it also includes "in addition—as even we cannot but feel—a clear overplus of meaning...."[15] It's not, in this conception of things, the absence of signs that causes us anxiety; rather, it's an excess of validation, the clicks and shocks of recognition that signal our creature feeling, the sense that "this" (the dream, the religious concept, the poem, life itself), as Finkelstein puts it, "It's an allegory, / a form of a form projected through time."[16] How does a poet handle the overplus of meaning that is the oceanic unconscious, while being tossed in energetic waves of the sacred? Carefully, as it happens, but bemusedly, transforming the overwhelming flood of feeling into something more manageable, specifically into a vision of things in hierarchical structure, intermediated by the office workers who

12. Eric L. Santner, *On the Psychotheology of Everyday Life* (Chicago: University of Chicago Press, 2001), 36.
13. Ibid., 39.
14. Rudolf Otto, *The Idea of the Holy*, translated by John W. Harvey (Oxford: Oxford University Press, 1958), 5.
15. Ibid.
16. Finkelstein, *Immanent Foundation*, 26.

occupy the structure. It's an ingenious transformation. Overwhelming dread changes into curiosity and bemusement.

Consider the poem "Dispatch," which concerns thousands of feet of film that have been discovered in an archive in the foundation, and the editing of which has been left to "others." These others— editors, perhaps? archivists, even? intermediaries, surely—engage in strange behavior that is described in the poem as "typical": "They eat the flowers, the ones on the plate / and the ones in the garden. They eat / the butterflies, and retell the story / of the famous boxer and his entourage."[17] However typical, these disruptions have come to the attention of the powers above in the hierarchy, who move toward clampdown:

> But if the board
> has its way, service will be disrupted
> across the entire network; free movement
> between the realms will cease; all of the
> passages previously interpreted will be
> returned to their original state of obscurity.[18]

The board having its way—presumably the anxiety about which prompts this dispatch to be sent in the first place—has three likely outcomes: service disruption; cessation of freedom of movement between the realms; and a collapse of interpreted clarities back into obscurity. "Network" is the great metaphorical word enabling the banality of the first statement. What percentage of office jargon is inherently poetic? Probably more than we'd like to admit. Service disruption alludes to a kind of magic—what network is meant here? Surely, one connected to the realms. This outcome belongs to the patently fantastical, one of Finkelstein's favorite kinds of literature to allude to. Furthermore, freedom of movement between the realms is an action that belongs to the greatest intermediaries of them all, the angels. (The word "hierarchy," referring to the rule or command of the sacred, was coined by Dionysius to characterize the orders of angels.) The

17. Ibid., 21.
18. Ibid.

third outcome brings us closest to the absorbing activity of Finkelstein's imagination: interpretation.

Freud calls dreams the "most mysterious of all instruments," insisting, "*The interpretation of dreams is the royal road to a knowledge of the unconscious activities of the mind.*"[19] In dreams, unconscious matter suppressed in obscurity comes mysteriously to life in nightly hidden narratives. Dream interpretation, which forms the core of Freudian psychoanalysis—you might even say its therapeutic application was Freud's principle innovation—is an unceasing chore. As soon as one dream's elements have been identified, it has been succeeded by a dozen more the patient has had in the interim. Dreaming is fractal—it proliferates even as it increases its density. This worried Freud, who wrote, "[T]he best way to complete the interpreting of a dream may be to abandon it in favour of the new dream, which recasts the same material in a form which may be more accessible."[20] There's a futility to all of this interpretation, and yet an efficacy, one in the therapeutic exchange that arises from familiarity. Soberly, even hopefully, Freud offers, "By far the most numerous kind of dream is one that rushes ahead of the treatment, so that, after everything that is already known and understood is abstracted from it, the dream provides a more or less clear indication of something that was previously hidden."[21]

It's from this mysterious but optimistic sweet spot Finkelstein's foundational dreams arise, rushing ahead of the Gnosis the poems serve (or, in office speak, are the Service Bureau of), clarifying hidden things. "Excess is Freud's theme," writes Adam Phillips. "Our desire, he tells us, is way in excess of any object's capacity to satisfy it; the meanings we make are in excess of the meanings we intend; our desire for death can be in excess of our desire for more life."[22] Finkelstein's *Immanent Foundation* institutionalizes the excesses of fantasy, both in

---

19. Sigmund Freud, *The Interpretation of Dreams,* trans. James Strachey (London: Penguin Books, 1991), 769.
20. Sigmund Freud, "On the Uses of Dream Interpretation in Psychoanalysis," in *Wild Analysis,* ed. Adam Phillips, trans. Alan Bance (London: Penguin Books, 2002), 16.
21. Ibid., 18.
22. Adam Phillips, "Introduction," *The Penguin Freud Reader,* ed. Adam Phillips (London: Penguin Books, 2006), ix.

the form of desire and in the generic literary form. The ingeniousness of these poems is the ease with which he merges these elements.

What enables this merge? In a word, *thaumaturgy*. It means "wonder-working." Its use in English starts during the Enlightenment. Finkelstein invokes it in "Novel," which begins:

> When the grindylow break into his cell
> he has already lost a hand, but this, apparently,
> is nothing compared to what they have in store
> for him.

Grindylow are magical creatures of the bog found in the Harry Potter books. They also appear in a China Miéville novel as well. While they may have folkloric origins, they're clearly the products of literary fantasy, which is the likeliest place Finkelstein encountered this word. And which, to make a full disclosure, is where I first encountered the word "thaumaturgy," almost certainly when I read Lyndon Hardy's novel *Master of the Five Magics*, published in 1980.[23]

"Novel" continues:

> They take him away in a bubble
> of air as the sea rushes through the portal.
> She hears the rattle of bones as the necklace
> of the grindylow magus shakes with each flicker
> of his tail.

Grindylow magus?! Finkelstein's "Novel" is magical fantasy populated with a hybrid mythical creature-magician. Part of the keen pleasure of these poems, especially for anyone who reads fantasy literature as well as poetry, is this ease with which Finkelstein merges these genres. He pushes on, blithely:

---

23. I will admit to rereading this novel recently, out of curiosity, in part, since it left an impact on my adolescent imagination when I first read it. I can safely report that the novel, which has a few good moments in it, and which does indeed introduce thaumaturgy to its readers, is not otherwise worth rereading, or even reading for that matter.

> This? It's a recording device,
> primitive but effective. No on/off switch.
> They're called pages. Yes, I suppose so,
> an interface. The floor is slick with blood.
> Thaumaturgical energy pulses through
> the corridor. This? It's an allegory,
> a form of a form projected through time.[24]

Thaumaturgy builds the visionary telescope of these poems, enabling their far-seeing intent. T. S. Eliot, writing about Dante, helpfully insists that "for a competent poet, allegory means clear visual images. And clear visual images are given much more intensity by having a meaning—we do not need to know what that meaning is, but in our awareness of the image we must be aware that the meaning is there too."[25] The form of the form projecting through time in these poems manifests to us in the excessive clear visual images of Finkelstein's language, as well as the smoky mirror of the interpreting intelligence brought to bear on the transmission of these images. What's novel about the Immanent Foundation is that the hidden narrative, in plain view before us, is the poem's thaumaturgy, the energy moving through the corridors, crossed by mercurial but helpful intermediaries, who lead to the hierarchical figures, themselves forms of a form projected through time, altogether constituting the poem's wonder-working power.

---

24. Finkelstein, 338.
25. T. S. Eliot, *Dante* (London: Faber & Faber, 1929), 22–3.

None of This Is Made Up: Norman Finkelstein and the Paranormal Postmodern

Joseph Donahue

> *Every natural effect has a spiritual cause.*
> —Blake (124)

epic tale

Here's a tale, an epic one: Once the world was ruled by magic, then it wasn't. So redacted, the tale lacks grandeur. But add some details, and a wealth of narratives spring up. Adding details is what, in this instance, academic disciplines do. Religion, psychology, history, literature, each tells a version of the tale. Sociology's is justly famous if dully titled: the secularization thesis. For Max Weber, the world ruled by magic is called enchanted, and was long ago; then came centuries of religious wars, orthodoxy, the state, science, the marketplace; and enchantment went away. Where, a listener might well wonder, did enchantment go? Some have said gone for good, turned into churches that offer little more than social services. Or, driven into psychotherapy, self-help, into the New Age niche markets of the spirit. Others say, go to the movies. Magic is utterly alive, there, ruling our imaginations to such a degree that we're shamed out of talking about it. So then, the now critically engaged auditor of the tale might ask: Does the relentless modern interest in the magical prove that it is still there, if only as the residue of what once was? Or is modern magic distinct, a phenomenon that arises within the ever-arriving secular world, and that may even, perversely, secure the way for the final rule of reason?

117

laws unknown

One recent rendering of the fate of magic in the modern world sets the tale in the late nineteenth century. For historian of religion Jeffrey Kripal this is the period when a prominent permutation of the term magic, the sacred, slips into the lexicon of science under the then new category of the paranormal. Researchers into psychic phenomenon wondered if such diverse activities as telepathy, astral projection, mediumistic communications from the dead, when subjected to scientific inquiry, might reveal the hidden laws governing appearance. In his study of what we might think of as the ever-modulating ratio of reason to magic in the late nineteenth and early twentieth century Euro-American culture, *Authors of the Impossible*, Kripal turns—somewhat surprisingly—not to religion or to the history of the social sciences but to literary criticism to understand the significance of what he would call "anomalous experience" in the modern world. In doing so he offers a point of entry to the reader of modern poetry curious about the pervasive discourse of the magical at work within poetry and poetics. The genre of the fantastic, hardly the premier mode of modernity, plays a rebellious role in the colonization by secularity of the world's belief systems. In our experience of the fantastic we live again in that older empire when magic ruled. Correspondences flourish. Copernicus never happened. The fantastic, Kripal argues, has immense critical value for scholars of religious thought who would understand the interrelation of reason and magic that persists within the modern secular world. The fantastic allows the formerly accepted but now rejected view that the world is ruled by magic to be considered at least momentarily plausible. A fantastic narrative will if well told ultimately ask the reader if the laws of the secular world, the world as understood through a scientifically based empiricism should remain as they are, so the fantastic can be dismissed as an illusion, or if in some real way the fantastic event has taken place, not, that is, as mere psychology. The reader is then pressed to accept the possibility that, as Kripal says, citing Todorov, "reality is controlled by laws unknown to us" (34).

paranormal postmodern

Impossible writing creates a duration within which the reader cannot decide if he or she is in a world of magic or a world of reason. Kripal calls this kind of writing the paranormal postmodern. The paranormal here has exceeded its origins as a term within the scientific inquiry into anomalous experiences. Further, the paranormal is an effect of reading as much as of undisclosed forces; it is as much about style as it is about science. Kripal's case studies of impossible writing are not novelists writing fantastic fiction, they are writers who record what is unbelievably real. Each would no doubt assert the fantastic arises not as a result of formal or stylistic innovations, but by attention to how the world works, though each would accept some version of the idea that a mode of writing is a mode of metaphysical inquiry. This, in my view, aligns them less with romancers, fabulists and realists that with the poets who were their contemporaries, particularly those poets who recognize as part of their art the cultivation of and depiction of visionary states of being, states that shape the writing as the writing itself intensifies the state. The poetry of any number of figures crucial to twentieth century poetics could be written by authors of the impossible. These texts constantly ask what laws govern reality, and devise methods of writing that allow the impossible to seem plausible. They call for poetry to create memorable imaginings of the limits of consciousness and self-understanding by allowing the reader to feel the worldview lurking within the manifestation of the poetic. In any number of late-nineteenth- and early- to mid-twentieth-century poets we can feel what it would mean to believe, in Blake's words, that natural effects have spiritual causes. Much modern poetry, after all, imagines its origins in a world ruled by magic, and, however deeply set within the regimen of reason, draws affective riches from these reclaimed origins. The history of poetry tells our epic tale, the world was enchanted, then it wasn't. Jerome Rothenberg's multi-volume anthology *Poems for the Millennium* gives rich witness to the interrelation of poetic form and religious thought from the Enlightenment to the present. Signal texts of twentieth-century poetics clearly place poetry in the domain of the paranormal postmodern: doctrines of inspiration, images, dreams, the logic of collage, selves hidden within selves, the spirit of death and lament rising up through the feet, devotional practices disguised as advice to the young, the poetic culture of modernity is rife with the kind of phenomenon one might find in any number of religious sub-cultures. Even the ever-evolving strategies of interpretation, the ritual acts of textual renewal that we call literary criticism, so often performed as skeptical acts of disenchantment, participate in the fantastic. Textual explication creates moments when the chastened reader can entertain the impossible as plausible. Even scholarship contributes to astonishment. Monumental scholarly editions restore some primordial text, or some ultimate text. Research is conjuring, as Susan Howe has demonstrated.

all such entities

Norman Finkelstein ongoing visionary satire of secularity and religion, "From the Files of the Immanent Foundation," is built upon the rock of a complexly rendered figure, one that precisely evinces the cultural hour of the waning of a magical world view that Kripal has turned to both in *Authors of the Impossible* and elsewhere. The hour, the late nineteenth century early twentieth century hour, brought us among much else symbolists, theosophy, psychoanalysis, Modernism, and the beginnings of the study of comparative religion. The figure of the Immanent Foundation is the satire's supreme fiction. Each of the poems that make up the larger poem is in some sense a file kept by a mysterious corporate entity that needs no Citizen's United to give it life. This fantasia upon the theme of corporate identity draws on the restructuring of social, political and financial life around new forms of social organizations in the early modern period. While I recognize that foundations are forms of corporate entity, and further, that corporations are institutions that are different from governments and churches, I point to Finkelstein's adjective as license to assume, within the world of the poem, a deep likeness that these forms of social organization share. Finkelstein has created a paradoxical and uncanny institution that sums up the life we all live: "As for the Foundation itself, it is not a governmental agency, not a sect or cult, not a fraternal organization, not a think tank, not a research institution—but I think it 'exists' in the spaces between and behind all such entities." (359) So the poet says, but the reader may well suspect that the Foundation "exists" in the spaces not just between and behind, but within these institutions, in all their various architectures. After all, it is immanent! And not only these public spaces but private spaces as well. Though what are we to make of the whole notion of privacy, of the conviction that some part of us is beyond the reach of collective identities?

The Foundation is the place that modernity provides to record, study, and provoke the anomalous experiences that Kripal places at the heart of the paranormal, and so at the heart of religion. However, the Foundation at first seems in the service of our sense of ourselves as rational and autonomous agents. It mimics in its protocols and procedures the methods of science, as if dedicated to the noble claim that spiritual effects have natural causes. The effect of this ritual mimicry, however, is the exact reverse. Through the course of the poem the Foundation validates Blake's assertion that natural effects have spiritual causes. As we read further into the poem we are kept by the interplay of perspectives at work from determining whether the Foundation means to repress or mainstream those anomalous experiences that persist in occurring even after the apparent demise of any supernatural world view. This incessant indecision compels the poem and the narratives told within it. Moreover, as we grasp Finkelstein's trope of modern sociality in the full measure of its uncanniness we cannot elude the suspicion that in our increasingly surveilled and regulated social world where churches become governments and governments become corporations and corporations are churches in disguise and all are bound by the language of family, that the Immanent Foundation is the foundation of all foundations.

The specter of Spicer

The poets of the Berkley Renaissance were good students and studied hard the emergence of the secular world from the older magical cosmos. Furthermore, they lived it. These poets met at the very site of programmatic disenchantment, the university, and created within it a series of magical social structures, beginning with the kries, a private devotional practice centered on the figure of the tragically dead poet, in this instance Stephan Georg. The Georg kries was just one of several iterations of an occult sociality formed by these poets around the veneration of poetry, which would come to include gatherings around the table of King Arthur, stray erotic encounters, and Magic Workshops. These poets reversed our epic tale. For them, the world was disenchanted, then it wasn't. Poetry transformed it. Finkelstein, though writing at a later moment, shares their faith in the magic of poetry in a secular age. "From the Files of the Immanent Foundation" is ultimately about the institution of poetry itself, or at least poetry that follows from the poets of the San Francisco Renaissance, poetry that arises from traditions of occult sociality: poetry as a counter institution, intensified in its magical ambitions by the increasing secularization of the modern world. A precursor to these poets William Butler Yeats prophesied the rise of the Immanent Foundation when he famously remarked: "I am very religious, and deprived by Huxley and Tyndall, whom I detested, of the simple-minded religion of my childhood, I had made a new religion, almost an infallible church, out of poetic tradition" (276).

Let's say Yeats is the first of three points on a graph that would trace the relation of magic to poetry in the modern and post-modern period. Yeats concentrates various traditions of wayward spirituality in the nineteenth century, most particularly the founding of a modern religion of theosophy. The second point appears on an arc that runs from Europe to America, and by America, I mean Berkeley. Here at midcentury Duncan, Spicer and Blaser received the traditions of esoteric European spirituality and bring to them their own understanding of magic as students of psychoanalysis, anthropology, linguistics, and popular culture. The magus of esoteric initiation, Orpheus, appears to Jack Spicer as Sophie Tucker. These poets begin writing at a significant moment in the transformations of western occulture (for an exploration of the term "occulture," see Christopher Partridge, *The Re-Enchantment of the West*, Vol. 1, Bloomsbury, 2005), mingling Old World hieratic cravings with a keen sense that the older world of American folk magic has never died, but has been reborn in modern media. The third point on the arc is Finkelstein's own post countercultural moment, which sees the promulgation of alternative spirituality in the New Age movement, as well as the unleashing of Christian fundamentalism in the political mainstream. Further, the hidden home in the academy for occult socialities is foreclosed by critical disinterest in discussions of spirituality, ritual and myth in regard to the visionary tradition that extends from Milton to Robert Duncan. Given on one hand the surge of rightwing fundamentalist rhetoric in the Reagan years and beyond, and on the other the easily derided mass marketing of once privileged discourses of mystic-erotic practice, Finkelstein could readily see what had come to be in the development of western occulture, the tendency of occult sociality to become institutionalized. Indeed, Finkelstein sees in his moment the impossibility of magical thought and practice apart from self-gathering collective entities that as Wallace Stevens would say rise like structures in the mist.

In addressing the state of magic in our time Finkelstein surveys the rogue metaphysics of burgeoning mythologies of the sacred. His attention in "From the Files of the Immanent Foundation" is sometimes on the anomalous experiences of the spiritually inclined individual, other times on the traumatized and abject sufferer, but always on the specific social structure that emerges to monitor and control any purported intrusions of the spirit. Finkelstein writes, after all, in the era, in the country, where corporations can claim personhood. This forthrightly atavistic turn in capitalist social organization suggests that they have already developed their own occult practice. if corporations are persons, they are entitled to their own rituals and beliefs, their own creeds, what certainly an anthropologist of "corporate culture" would recognize as distinct religious formations. (Go, test the truth of the poem on your own pulse. Read it, then enter an insurance office, a hospital, a university, a registry of motor vehicles, go to Apple for a phone upgrade. Watch the workings of our world, the minions with their rituals that so control our lives.) In response to his historical moment, Finkelstein depicts the fuller place of the paranormal in modern life. In doing so he presents us not only with a history of the place of magic in the rule of reason, but shows us a history that goes back to the origins of secularity itself. The Immanent Foundation encodes and markets the lore of those earlier esotericisms, and the devotion to them of artistic coteries, both early in the century in Europe, and at midcentury in the poetry of the San Francisco Renaissance. As the poem unfolds the reader enters still further realms of wondrous beliefs, most notably the premodern world of European folk culture, and the fantastic imaginative investments made in it by secular art cultures. And as the United States is currently in the midst of a recurrence of blood and soil mysticism that calls up the less endearing side of European occultism, those strains which aligned themselves with fascism, we can sense a keen political wherewithal that leads the poem to touch upon the psychological origins of totalitarianism.

"From the Files of the Immanent Foundation" is not simply a fantasia on secularity's emergence from the dark depths of an older religious world, it is a study of the increasingly complex interrelation of states of enchantment and disenchantment within modernity. Finkelstein builds multiple poems within the larger suite around the dream of a science of the anomalous. Its science is spooky. Scenarios involving testing, evidence, repeatable results, psychological evaluations, are part of reason's dream of subjugating magic to its laws. Finkelstein calls up the early twentieth century understanding of magic as the beginning of science. As Fraser suggests in a work so crucial to modern poetry, *The Golden Bough*, early magical practices encode the notion of universal laws. A substrate of imagery running through the poem suggests the whole history of what philosophers and anthropologists saw as the yet to be established science of mythology. Should that list of Immanent Foundation founders ever be made public among them as well as Frazer might be Cassirer, Warburg, Freud, Jung, Frederik Meyer, William James along with Andrew Lang, Lady Wilde, the Brothers Grimm. Perhaps more crucial than any of these would be the poet Jack Spicer, who shows us the other side of the scientizing of magic. Our rhetoric becomes magic, then magic controls our words. "My vocabulary did this to me." Spicer haunts the hallways of the Foundation as he does the lines of Finkelstein's poetry. He is the most compelling of the tellers of our epic tale, how could he not be? His work records how magic killed him. When one considers Finkelstein's long standing critical and poetic interest in Spicer, the influx of dictated material that enters into his previous collection *Inside the Ghost Factory*—yet another iteration of the relation between institutions and the unconscious—one cannot help but hear Spicer's final words lurking behind the Foundations proselytizing pitch. For Spicer, the poem becomes the force that governs fate. One would seem free to choose the vocabulary, but the process of becoming a poem, of beginning in the disenchantment of modernity and entering into the world of magic, reenacts the enlightenment in reverse. Words become not just magical but themselves divine, bequeathing death on their devotee. His reputed final words replicate Spicer's own tormented awareness of the interrelation of reason and magic throughout all his writing. (Certainly, the *Collected Books* are hidden away in a well-guarded vault of the Immanent Foundation.) Spicer was both sceptic and devotee. He both tormented and energized the interrelated states of reason and magic, at the behest of making the impossible temporarily plausible. No poet of the New American dispensation so twisted our epic tale with every line. The world vacillates between disenchantment and enchantment at terrific speed. Poetic form arises from and encodes this vacillation. As a poet of both satire and terror Spicer is the daemon wandering the hallways of the Immanent Foundation. He belittles spiritual longings, then he embodies them. Drawing Yeats out of his Swiss grave Spicer unleashes a poetry of dictation into the postwar poetics which Finkelstein continues. "From the Files of the Immanent Foundation" asks what we do now with what magic was then, both in Yeats time, and in Spicer's time.

And in our own. Beneath its elegance and invention, the poem draws on the intoxicating promise of mythological syncretism and new religious revelation that characterized the occult sociality in Yeats' time. It draws on a pained spiritual awareness of the fraught quality of the occult sociality, and on the disruptive power of the daemonic that is everywhere in Spicer's work. As a visionary satire, the poem marks a distance from midcentury magic, picking up on and furthering Spicer's own ambivalent wit in regard to recreating magic in the realm of reason. The Immanent Foundation is the Magic Workshop, incorporated and franchised. The séance table is now the board room. Queer Knights of the Round Table are now clients; messages from Mars are now memos from management. The fate of Spicer haunts the poem, the fate of one for whom poetry becomes an institution with complete control over life. The destructive displays of the paranormal recorded in Finkelstein's poem are his attempt to reckon with Spicer's ghost. The compulsive retelling of paranormal experience which is the method of Finkelstein's poem, the way each file draws upon the conventions of the supernatural story-telling, telling the same story in different words file after file bespeaks a poet aware of the deathly treachery of a vocabulary marked as his. The cool of narrative conventions is the spell that protects Finkelstein, the contemporary poet of magic and reason, from death by lyric vocabulary.

Then cherish pity

Banks, academies, businesses, hospitals, guilds, political parties, the police, the IRS, municipal, county, state and federal government, financial markets, transnational corporations, private security firms, perhaps, though we will never know for sure, what has been termed the "deep state," in calling the Immanent Foundation a "foundation," the poet places his figuration of occult sociality in the legal and historical landscape of modern institutions. Foundations are part of the epic tale of the transition of the world from magic to reason: they arose in a world once ruled by the church, but then, after centuries of religious wars, it wasn't. Foundations, those, that is, with pretense to charitable purpose, were part of the turning of the common life from a religious to a secular world order. Where agape was, the enlightenment decreed, philanthropy shall be. The founding word of charitable foundations, those which established the class of what we understand today as foundations, derived not from any gospel but from the classical paradigm of selfless and divine and tormented giving, it's what Aeschylus

called Prometheus: "human loving." Through philanthropy the state
sponsored fellow-feeling, and, coincidentally, urged the amelioration
of social conditions that might otherwise threaten its rule. In a yet to
be collected file Finkelstein nods to this history. The foundation, he
tells us, was built on the ruins of love. Finkelstein, ever acute in his
ironies, summons, here and elsewhere, a witness to the interpenetrating
polarities of reason and magic at work in an earlier point in the emergence
of the secular and the diminution of the religious, William Blake.
Blake's visionary satires are the founding charters of the Immanent
Foundation. They, too, query the transformation of spiritual, erotic,
and civic love. Finkelstein's deepest debt to Blake, as we will see, shows
itself in the way "From the Files of the Immanent Foundation" presents
contrary states of the soul. However, it is in regard to the establishment
of philanthropy as a legal and cultural part of secular society that the
first specific echo of Blake occurs. In the "Songs of Innocence" Blake
depicts the spectacle of philanthropic magnanimity presenting itself as
a modern form of Christian charity. In "Holy Thursday" wards of the
state are marched into church for the edification of devout citizens:

> O what a multitude they seemd these flowers of London town
> Seated in companies they sit with radiance all their own
> The hum of multitudes was there but multitudes of lambs
> Thousands of little boys & girls raising their innocent hands
>
> Now like a mighty wind they raise to heaven the voice of song
> Or like harmonious thunderings the seats of Heaven among
> Beneath them sit the aged men wise guardians of the poor
> Then cherish pity, lest you drive an angel from your door (13)

Among the first people we meet when we arrive at the Foundation
are the descendants of these orphans: "... The orphans are seated /
in the chapel, each one holding a rose. Some have been / taught to sing"
(318). The singing orphans are part of the pitch the Foundation makes.
Wastrels on display starkly announce the theme of social relations.
Unlike those sanctimonious churchgoers who well know where they
are, and have some notion, though certainly not Blake's, of what they

are seeing, readers of Finkelstein have no such hypocritical confidence. They are not in a church. It's not quite clear where they are. In such wise does the Foundation work its will on readers of the poem. We continually wonder what our relation to the Foundation is. Who are we, that a messenger arrives amid our disenchantment, and escorts us to a meeting? How parodic, if at all, is this send-up of spiritual election? Are we apostles? Prospective members? Clients? Customers? Initiates? Students? Analysands? Worshipers? Donors? Future employees? Deeper into the poem we will ask are we persons at all, or just passing inhabitants of eternal states, immanent ourselves, never feeling fully manifest in our lives? And where in the modern secular world, in the opening poems, do we find ourselves, such selves as we might have to find or be found? Blake had a London of foreign wars, mercantilism, universal rights, sex magic, and the slave trade from which to fashion his own immanent foundation, Golgonooza. Finkelstein's chartered streets are harder to find on a materialist map. They could be in Vienna, New York, or Cincinnati. The lack of locale is in keeping both with Finkelstein's commitment to the imagination and with the nature of modern-day corporate headquarters, where the architecture has no need to accommodate congregations and sacramental practices, and is invested in not reflecting the particular location of the office. Walk into an office of a multi-national corporation anywhere in the world and the office is where you are, not the place in the world where the office is. As "From the Files of the Immanent Foundation" makes clear, the occult double of the Foundation, the corporation, exercises far more subtle influence over our daily lives than did Saint Paul's over the congregants of London. As we will see, social institutions of all kinds are on the poet's mind in his satire on the place of religious sentiment in secularity. What for Blake was primarily the interrelation of church and state at an earlier moment of the evolution of institutions becomes a proliferation of overlapping institutions that control our sense of who we are. And which win or hold our allegiance through a variety of magical practices.

contraries

While we may know less about the Immanent Foundation than we do about churches, governments, rotary clubs and day care centers, we know it offers what such do not: magical powers. Touring the corporate campus, we might feel we are curious and conscientious consumers, deciding whether to invest in such magic as seems to be readily available. Yet the initial offer contains some fine print.

The magic made available may include such side effects as the daemonic, the psychical, the paranormal, the occult, the psychotic. Whatever we call the invisible forces that are presumed to link mind and matter begin to display themselves the longer we linger. Still, we are not recruited, not converted, we are invited in, shown around. We participate in social protocols. We are prompted to feel we are autonomous rational selves, albeit mildly depressed, browsing one particular outlet in the spiritual marketplace that has arisen in the west since the Second World War. As soon as we step onto the grounds we are told "rhetoric becomes magic" (314). This initial characterization of magic does not require contact with the inner life of the practitioner. However even here, in the opening pitch, a link between the magician and the magic suggests itself. Rhetoric, after all, can bend the external world to one's will with no real semblance of supernatural agency. The Immanent Foundation has the demographics of the disenchanted in its data base, and knows the appeal of easy access spiritual technology. No creeds or doctrines needed, no vestige of traditional religious interiority would seem to be active anywhere on the grounds.

The Immanent Foundation as it comes to present itself to the reader is an embodiment of contraries. The contraries are not Innocence and Experience, but Reason and Magic. Blake had advised Finkelstein that a visionary work must commit itself to a perspective that arises from seeing each state in terms of its own logic, and also seeing each state as implicit in its contrary. The opening poems of "From the Files of the Immanent Foundation" explore different ratios of reason to magic at work, in each poem as a whole, in particular images, and most especially in the individual sentence. Those poems we might consider "Songs of

Reason" present magic as a skill, as a technology, as a means of control, as professional codes one can master and be successful. They are the world as seen by a sociologist of religion. The "Songs of Magic" depict a contrary world of mysteries, anomalous events, dreams, hallucinations, fantastic accounts, credulity and wonder. It is the world of those who are within magic, those for whom natural effects have spiritual causes. They are the world as seen by an anthropologist who's taken the peyote and become a shaman. Among the "Songs of Reason" we find codes, technologies, rhetoric, ceremonies, fame based on performances, a lever that can be pulled to reveal the other side, sacred roles determined by algorithms, and a still largely effective incest taboo. The "Songs of Reason" are peopled by midlevel spiritual bureaucrats celebrating the exteriorization of the psychic. By contrast, the "Songs of Magic" feature a different experience of magic and, most crucially for the poem, a different tone. The "Songs of Magic" are peopled by initiates, victims, by those losing their shit. Buildings burn down and disappear. A figure seems to ascend to heaven. An oracular Master speaks in his sleep. Angels are evoked. Folkloric phenomena abound. Medieval worlds seem to be still in progress. What is promoted is a disposition of awe, and submission to wonders and terrors. Some poems, such as "Lab Report," survey the state of magic as understood within the state of reason. Others seem precisely the inverse. It is not the sacrosanct division of these states of the soul that propels the poem, however, but their interpolation within a single sentence. Through the vacillating ironies of the sentence Finkelstein explores and anatomizes modern religious passion. His sentences announce him an Author of the Impossible. The vacillation of these states, Reason and Magic, continually interrogate causality. Do natural effects have spiritual causes, or spiritual effects have natural causes? Readers are led, poem after poem, to hesitate in judging what laws are at work in what they are reading. Each file from the Immanent Foundation accomplishes the continuous reinvention of the plausible.

Egypt

A key source for the poem (358), Eric Santner's *Psychotheology of Everyday Life* gives a twist to our epic tale: the world will be ruled by magic not until it is not but until it is so more beneficently. The teller spins us around. The secular world turns out to be the oldest kind of magic: Egyptian magic. (Did you think the Enlightenment had freed you from the bonds of superstition? Think again. Even after deconstruction you are still a spellbound slave in ancient Egypt.) Secularity, in this telling, is a form of religion that disguises itself as the triumph of reason over religion. Santner sets his meditation on the place of institutional authority in modern life within an all-encompassing trope of magic. For Santner also there are also two contrary states, but both are zones of magic: the cursed and the blessed. Secularity is magic that disguises itself as reason. We think we are rational and free but we are cursed. Our modern institutions maintain the curse. They regulate out "symbolic identities." Our doom is our attachment to the "dignities of personhood" which are bestowed by our institutions, even if those institutions present themselves as religious, or if they appear to us within the myth of a private life as our families. What is needed, Santner argues, is not a disenchanting application of reason to our religious beliefs, but a truer religion. (For him, this is a Judaism shaped by psychoanalysis and critical theory.) Only a truer religion will get us out of the Egypt of modern life. Santner switches good magic for bad. His espousal of a life given to immanence rather than afflicted by transcendence is in the end a travail and an entrance into a promised land, where we are offered "more life." We leave the land of bans and enter the land of blessings. Santner, however, confirms Finkelstein's insight, and Blake's, about the prominence of institutions, both in our social lives and in our psychic lives, as well as in the translation of an older religious world view into a secular one. Further, he broadens the implications of Finkelstein's anatomy of the paranormal. He confirms that secular institutions remake the magical world view for modernity. He also confirms that in modernity we are living lives that mirror Blake's doctrine of contrary states, which is to say that while we are tormented

131

in Egypt and are free in Zion, we are not free of Egypt when we reach the land of Zion. We live perpetually with an Egypt that takes the form of the unconscious of others. Finkelstein in turn endorses Santner's depiction of our condition, that our symbolic identities are governed by institutions in ways we are invested in not seeing, to preserve our sense of ourselves as rational, free agents. Finkelstein proposes that it is poetry not Judaism that has the power to free us of this unhappy state. freedom is, again, not a freedom from magical thought, but a modification of it. Poetry does not disenchant us, though it does allow is to see ways by which we are unhappily enchanted. Further, poetry shows that disenchantment is itself a spell cast over reason.

However, it is unclear to what degree Finkelstein's fiction of The Immanent Foundation shows us a way out of Egypt, or validates our enslavement. While I have suggested that the Foundation can be read as about the institution of poetry as the poet has inherited it from Jack Spicer, Finkelstein's ironies are inescapable, and in an infernal way which both Spicer and Blake would appreciate. The Foundation may itself be immanent, but what kind of immanence lends itself to being so pliant to human forms? Santner proposes immanence as a state of holiness, as what life will be like in the perpetual Sabbath of life after a successful psychoanalysis. A true Immanent Foundation would be a synagogue or a psychoanalytic institute. Yet Finkelstein's ironies place us in a world of dystopic sci-fi. An immanent foundation is itself a contrary state, or a contradiction that suggests a contrary state. Since what can immanence mean beyond the uncanniness Finkelstein ascribes to it? The philosophical implication of the adjective would require it to have a source beyond the mediation of human social structures. Immanence implies a totality which includes the human world but exceeds it. Certainly, Santner sees immanence in this fashion, it is a communion with the divine order as it makes itself known to the properly perceiving soul. Perhaps the Immanent Foundation is in its way a marriage of heaven and hell. A Foundation that offers immanence? An immanence that can only per experienced through the protocols of a modern secular institution. As if we were forever in the world of Scientology? Is part of Finkelstein's impossible writing to continually forestall the readers determination as to whether or not he or she is cursed or blessed? This might be the case, a world of contrary states, the world as it was had Blake only written the "Songs of Innocence and Experience,"or if Blake had only written parts of "The Marriage of Heaven and Hell," if Blake had not then integrated the doctrine of contrary states into his emerging prophetic imagination.

Non-Entity

Writing in the tradition of Blake, drawn like Blake to imagining a world ordered by contrary states, Norman Finkelstein takes the measure of our transcendental desires. Finkelstein's own specter, Eric Santner, has arisen like a blue mist from the poet's foot and confirmed that Blake's apprehensions about the coercive power of a deeply entwined church and state is applicable, in our time, to all the institutions that shape our sense of ourselves for us. Only an illusion created by the state of Reason leads us to feel we feel we know ourselves apart from them. Finkelstein would undo the rituals of symbolic investiture at work in the Egypt of all our institutions. He does this not by offering a poetry of disenchanted secularism but by daemonizing all levels of institutional life. "From the Files of the Immanent Foundation" continually reenacts the attempt of institutional authorities, who often speak in the poem in tones of personal management, to control the anomalous experiences of the individual, until, as the poem draws to a close, these authorities surrender the discourses of reason and speak frankly in terms of enchantment. As a poem of the impossible, "From the Files of the Immanent Foundation" is consecrated to moments of the fantastic. With help from Santner we can see that the state of Reason, which the Immanent Foundation promotes with its sales pitch of scientific inquiry and rational mastery of invisible forces, is erroneously understood as opposing magic in the way that the secularization thesis, our epic tale, would tell it. The world was enchanted then it wasn't, reveals itself to be, in the course of Finkelstein's version, the world wants you to believe that it is disenchanted, and the world will use a new form of modern magic to make it appear so. The deep ironies at work in Finkelstein's trope of the Immanent Foundation complicate a pressing question: is it a purveyor of good or bad magic? Are we in the hellish world of experience, where melancholy, madness, and foundational maleficence dissolve the imperiled self, or are we in the heavenly world of rational bliss, where skills and know-how and institutional credentials enhance our illusions of freedom and choice?

Without contraries is no progression; does the Foundation show its clients, its adepts, or the poet who called them all before us, a level of understanding beyond the contraries that are the lifeblood of the Foundation? With the presumably complete text of Finkelstein's poem now in hand, a possible further development of the doctrine of contrary states suggests itself. This development is not necessarily within the poem, but at its perimeters. Consider how Blake himself moved from visionary satires to prophecies, how the voice of the Bard which sounds within the world of contraries is brought forward in the succession of genres. The new genre of prophecy demands the doctrine of states be developed beyond what we see in Innocence and Experience. Notable here is that most terrifying and profound state, Non-Entity. Non-Entity as Blake imagined it is social death on an astral plane. It is the ultimate curse that can fall upon a Zoa or its emanation. It is sung of in the prophecies with a fearful eloquence. It is how an Eternal experiences death. The Immanent Foundation does not imagine and populate an eternal realm, but it does record rumors of an eternal world, and legends of ascent and descent, keeping all the while a proper secular distance from the beyond. Daemonic forces are most often proven to be subject to human actions and human desires. The poem delights in pulling apart the voices of institutional authority that seek to measure and make use of psychic upheavals. But certain files take us beyond the perspectival play of contraries to where some whole other drama is welling. In these files Finkelstein forsakes the satiric unravelling of the language and posture of mastery. This occurs most dramatically around the disappearance of an early character, Margaret. Paired with Lucy, she, the deeply concealed sacrificial logic of the poem suggests, must die so that Lucy can live. Her file is notable for the refusal of the Foundation to address her destruction. She has entered Non-Entity, the "deathful infinite." Were she to speak, could the poem accommodate such a lament, she would be as eloquent as Enion singing:

> What is the price of experience? Do men buy it for a song,
> Or wisdom for a dance in the street? No, it is bought with the price
> Of all a man hath, his house, his wife, his children.
> Wisdom is sold in the desolate market where none come to buy,
> And in the withered field where the farmer ploughs for bread in
> vain. (325)

A second file goes further in the state of Non-Entity, providing us with one of the poem's great moments of pathos and visionary intelligence. In "Encounter" the poet lets drop the perspective that drives so much of the poem, the perspective of a faux scientific authority seeking to merchandize the incommensurable. Here neither science nor psyche can define the phenomenon. Here Finkelstein takes us further into the states that are lurking beneath the contraries of Reason and Magic. This poem presents an encounter with some other order of being, an afterlife that seems beyond any of the magic on sale by the Foundation, that seems beyond the ken of corporate consciousness. As such it marks a turn in Finkelstein's figuration of the place of magic in modern life. This file hints at a cosmology beyond that proposed by either Magic or Reason. In it we see, following Blake's example, the emergence of the prophetic voice, as the voice of the Bard in the *Songs of Innocence and Experience* anticipates the voice of the prophecies.

The encounter described in "Encounter" depicts a range of experience that seems beyond the means of the Foundation to regulate. We seem at the threshold of the symbolic identities that social institutions regulate. Perhaps this itself an illusion, the illusion that illusions come to an end. The poem here postulates a state of non-entity some utmost point that marks the outer limit of a conceivable world and records the process of entering into non-Entity. The poem notes two collective identities meeting and merging. The speakers become the others they encounter, we may not be wrong to assume that the others have become the speakers. It is the establishing of two realms and of beings in each real who are versions of each other, (much

135

as the Zoas are both eternal and fallen into the realm of even more doubling, Zoa and emanation, Zoa and specter ...) The two groups are stripped of the ways in which they might assess who and what they are. Non-Entity here is not the occasion for the arias of desolation that characterize Blake's renderings, yet Finkelstein remains true to how Non-Entity would appear within a visionary satire that explores contrary states. Those encountered seem to be from a beyond different from that proposed by either the state of Reason or the state of Magic. They may be those the Foundation has disappeared; they may be the ancestral dead, they may be something like Blakean emanations; their ontological status is of less poetical concern than the mood they usher into the poem. They bring a feeling of the effacement of self, of a loss that will not be recompensed within the logic of the poem. Finkelstein invokes a realm beyond the terror and wit and narrative invention of his poem. The state of Non-Entity is summoned by the very nature of the foundation itself, which has the power to curse as well as bestow blessings. But Non-Entity seems beyond it, and to encompass it, as when certain of Blake's songs rise to the rhetoric of the prophecies and suggest imaginative possibilities and expressive intensities beyond what the figures within the song perceive. "Encounter" explores the phenomenology of an occult sociality; we feel ourselves becoming part of a collectivity that is coming and going at once. We are doubled and diminished. Readers of the poet's other works might justly be tempted to read in this encounter a meditation on the holocaust. The evocations of Jewish folk materials and the persistent feel of the lost universe of European pre-war culture recall a whole population consigned to Non-Entity, and residing there, that Jews of a later moment might bond with them in psychic communion, and keep them alive within the living, just as the dead for their part might assure the living that they are already dead and united with their forbearers in eternity.

this magic moment

"Files from the Immanent Foundation" tells its own multi-perspectival tale of the fate of enchantment in the modern world. It brings to the fore the often-concealed prominence of magical thinking in the operations of the institutions that regulate our symbolic identities. As an enduring instance of the paranormal postmodern, the poem allowing readers to trade the impossible for the plausible. For the duration of that deal, natural effects have spiritual causes. Intuitions of a cosmological order—within which the contraries of reason and magic make their sense-making claims—arrive in waves of delight. As an historian of transcendental desires Finkelstein follows the fate of religiosity from the late nineteenth century to the present, from the Society of the Golden Dawn, to the Institute for Psychical Research, to mind science, occultism, and the permutation of vernacular spirituality to be found alike in critical theory and cable television shows. As a poet, he translates into the contemporary moment an earlier generation's anthropologically mediated reenactments of our epic tale, when an ethno-poet, dutifully apprenticed to ancient and pre-literate materials, would fervently summon the lost world of the magical. Finkelstein sees that magic is not just the transformative and potentially healing effects of charisma and incantation experienced by those gathered around the shaman, whose suffering re-enchants the present. Magic, for Finkelstein, is the law of any social gathering, and is at work in whatever the modern institution might be. The secular is the strongest spell ever cast; so runs Finkelstein's telling of the tale, a telling rich in wit, erudition, spiritual cravings, and narrative gifts.

Works Cited:

Blake, William. *The Complete Poetry and Prose of William Blake*, Ed. David V. Erdman, Anchor Books, 1988.

Finkelstein, Norman. *The Ratio of Reason to Magic*, Dos Madres, 2016.

Howe, Susan. *Spontaneous Particulars, The Telepathy of Archives*, New Directions, 2014.

Kripal, Jeffrey J. *Authors of the Impossible*, The University of Chicago Press, 2010.

Yeats, W. B., p 276, *The Yeats Reader*, Ed. Finneran, Scribner Poetry, 1997.

MIDRASH

Henry Weinfield [HW], Peter O'Leary [PO'L],
Mark Scroggins [MWS], Michael Heller [MH],
Ariel Resnikoff [AR], Eric Selinger [ES], Maeera Shreiber [MS]

It is the task of the translator to release in his own language that pure language that is under the spell of another, to liberate the language imprisoned in a work in his re-creation of that work.

Walter Benjamin, "The Task of the Translator" [AR]

(But not the priest in prayer of white marble, the tangled streets and knotted eyes supplicate in some grey clouded way, the raveled sea) And solitude, unbroken to the window

George Oppen [MH]

Even though the first tablets were broken, their sanctity obligates one not to treat them with contempt.

Berachot 8b:7 [MS]

#

The myth a record
of translation or transgression

COULD NOT
TRANSFER IMAGE
FROM [MH]

A scandal among the scribes
translating the myth

We know how to recount many falsehoods like real things, and We know how to proclaim truths when we wish.

Hesiod, Theogony, II. 27-8
to recount = *logein* (*legos*) >>
falsehood (*pseudea*)
to proclaim / to tell =
mythēsasthai (*mythos*) >>
truth (*alēthea*) …
logos >> false
myth >> true; i.e., "a scandal
among the scribes" [PO'L]

Recording the transgressions
of the schools and parties

traduttore, traditore (translator, traitor) [ES]

*Here the record
is broken and lost.*

#

At some point the record
was spirited away

In his influential essay "Redemption Through Sin" (1937) ["Mitzvah ha-Ba'ah be-Averah" : "The commandment that is fulfilled through its transgression"], Scholem argues that the Sabbatean "Mystery of the Godhead" was "nothing less than the totally unexpected revival of the religious beliefs of the ancient gnostics, albeit in a transvalued form."

David Biale, *Gershom Scholem: Kabbalah and Counter-History* [ES]

Spirited Away (2001), dir.
Hayao Miyazaki (?) [MWS]

At some point the spirit
was taken away

"Called Back" —Emily Dickinson's headstone
"Called forth" —cf Genesis 12:1
[ES]

Called forth, called away
Summoned or stolen

Temple or archive
Loss of the prepositions.

The Poem is source and translation.
Avot Yeshurun [AR]

"Archive" >> from *ta archeia* (public records)
from *arkhē* (government; beginning, source
of action, origin); cf "archaic," cf "archai" [ES]

141

Write it in this name with beautiful ink,
with a beautiful quill of an expert scribe,
and wrap the scroll in beautiful silk fabric
Shabbat 133b:5 [MS]

From where you came
—From a putrid drop; where
are you going—to a place
of dust …

From whence you go
to where you come
I won't arrive
at any place.
Avot Yeshurun, "All who come there"
[AR]

—Ethics of the Father, Ch. 3
[AR]

These directions
to or from the archive
to or from the temple
cannot be reconstructed
cannot be translated
cannot be

The tomb in Palenstine
Is not the porch of spirits lingering
Stevens, "Sunday Morning" [MWS]

Can teach us nothing
though the spirit lingers.

My scribe was a father
like all the scribes before him

"…the more familiar something is, the
stranger it becomes to unsettling us.
Peter O'Leary [MH]

#

Enamored in spirit….
[PO'L]

My father was a scribe
like his father before him

Enamored of the spirit
like his father before him

But the scriptures can teach us
            nothing though
the spirit lingers
In a place where we
may no longer go.

My father was a wandering
Aramean. [ES]

… the supreme divine power
undertook an endeavor, and failed
to carry it out.
Joseph Dan on Lurianic Kabbalah [MH]

"A place," not "The Place" (Ha-Makom)
which is a God-name. For "a" vs. "the,"
see Zukofsky, perhaps. [ES]

142

Black fire on the surface of
white fire
textualization = arcanization
detextualization = crisical
arcanization [PO'L]

(The long I sound drops away)
[ES]

last evening in my room
*   the life of a spirit*
A long-lived one, revealed
*   itself to us —*
why and when? — like a
*   flower in early spring*
shoots sunbound in Petal
-fold bouquet
  Mikhl Likht, P:VI [AR]

a disaster in the mother's tongue
her words emptied
by speaking …
Jerome Rothenberg, "In the
Dark World, Khurbn" [AR]

#

In a place where we
may no longer write

In a place about which
we may no longer write

Families of scribes
grown into tribes

Inspired
by an absent spirit.

#

Sign for 'folded tent"
translated as 'journey"

Signs for 'sea," "tablet" and "wall"
translated as 'archive"

Signs for 'sky, " "tablet" and "wall"
translated as "temple"

Sign for 'Journey"
translated as "scribe."

For "absent," read "absinthe."
The spirit that gives its name
to Artemesia absinthium
(wormwood)
Artemesia / who lives across
the ranges / stretching for
miles, / she's always there …
Gary Snyder, *Mountains &*
Rivers Without End [ES]

Not the forms but the forces.
Buber [MH]

The bridge between ought and is in
Judaism is ethics.
S. Handelman [MH]

143

Spell casting is an indispensable art;
it should rightly be held in high esteem,
and studied earnestly and thoroughly.
[PO'L]

The blessings and curses were recited
alternately, first one blessing and
then one curse.
Sotah 37b:11 [MS]

Hyperbole ! de ma mémoire
Triomphalement ne sais-tu
Te lever, aujourd'hui grimoire
Dans un livre de fer vêtu…

Hyperbole! can you not rise
In triumph from my memory,
A modern magic spell devise
As from an ironbound grammary.
Mallarmé, the opening lines of
"Prose." [HW]

Every place where I have my name
mentioned, I shall come to you and
bless you….
Exodus 20:21 [AR]

##

All spells recalled
but still accountable

Lost glamour, lost grammar
but still accountable

Lost gramarye.

#

Lost grimoire:

Soul-eater possibly
put to rest

Or never put to rest
now that all is lost.

#

"Only the faithful
hold this place green"

The magic withdrawn
the book dismembered

And the blessings and curses of the Lord.

A *grimoire* in French is a book of (magic) spells. Finkelstein in these sections is partly drawing on Mallarmé's poems "Ouverture Ancienne d'Hérodiade" (Ancient Overture of Hérodiade) and "Prose pour des Esseintes" (Prose for des Esseintes), along with the translation of and commentaries on these poems by Henry Weinfield, where *grimoire* is translated as *grammary* (Finkelstein has nicely changed the spelling to gramarye). A *prosa* is a Latin hymn, and Mallarmé's *prosa* is both a hymn and the antithesis of poetry (thereby signaling the loss of poetry). For Mallarmé, magic and poetry are metonymically linked; and so for Finkelstein the loss of the spells of magic associated with poetry is tantamount to a lost grammar and a lost glamour. In the opening line, "All spells recalled," "recalled" means both *remembered* and *called again* as well as *called back* (i.e., annulled). See Stéphane Mallarmé, *Collected Poems*, trans. Henry Weinfield (Berkeley, 1974), pp. 27, 46, 171–76, 192–96. [HW]

144

In the first volume of Tolkien's *Lord of the Rings*, the wizard Gandalf falls with the Balrog from the bridge of Khazad-dûm (*The Fellowship of the Ring* 11.5). In Ursula K. LeGuin's *The Farthest Shore*, the archmage Ged (Sparrowhawk) pursues his adversary Cob into the land of the dead. [MWS]

Nevertheless, at this very moment these same words, and a great many others like them, are being lost in language—and it does not matter. We are inwardly almost untouched. The core is consumed and their spiritual strength fades or is hidden, and only their husks, cast but from the private domain to the public, still persist in language, doing slack service within the limited boundaries of logic and social intercourse….
—H. N. Bialik, *Revealment and Concealment in Language* [AR]

me here, me, who can tell you all this, could have and don't and didn't tell you; me with a turk's-cap lily on my left, me with corn-salad, me with my burned candles, me with the day, me with the days, me here and there, me maybe accompanied—now—by the love of those I didn't love, me on the way to myself, up here.

\#   Celan [MH]

Gone in an instant
gone into the dance

Gone into the abyss
the wizard and his foe

All power drained away.

\#

Sexual potency
replacing the spells

Replacing the names

Soul and soul-eater
yielding to the flesh.

necromancy
chiromancy
hyrdromancy
psychophagy
psychoanalysis
[PO'L]

145

##

They were invested
in that magic

So was I

They were invested
in that language.

#

Was there any choice?

Yes, the world answered:
here is pain and beauty
in equal measure

Equal to any magic.

#

Or another order
of the same magic?

Here at the cabin
chipmunks, chickadees

So close to hand.

146

A cage went in search of a bird.
Kafka [MH]

Not *pleasure as full-throated ease*
[ES]

#

So close one can only
react with pleasure

The dis-ease of pleasure
pleasure of dis-ease

The jay squawking in the aspens.

The crows in morning
bringing food
from source to source
to the hatchlings

#

The jay squawking
asking for more

This one fills
and this one lfits
This one fills
and this one lifts
Avot Yeshurun, "The House"
[AR]

More magic
in the simplicity of its hunger

Than the poem can sustain.

Jay, in the family Cervidae, including magpies, crows, and ravens too, highly intelligent birds. Given the aspens, western trees, most likely then the Western Scrub-Jay, to be found in Colorado, whose noise, according to Sibley, is "generally harsh and angry-sounding." A handsome bird—*Aphelocoma californica.*
[PO'L]

147

##

And yet the poem
must sustain all things

All of the orders
as have been prescribed

As have been ordered.

#

Therefore and
therefore

Not-that it can be explained
not that it can be inscribed

But still.

#

Nor is language magic
as in some cabal
waving their wands

Not magic but mystery
into which one may go.

148

#

Into which one may go
when one's name is called

Called by the Name
the nameless Name

Called into the nameless.

#

Not mystification
but a simple mystery

The self and the world
are made manifest in language

Called out of the nameless.

149

##

cf. "The dis-ease of
pleasure / pleasure
of dis-ease"
[ES]

But why am I called
to use *this* language?

So wise, she said
putting me ill at ease
troubling the waters.

cf. Genesis 1.2 [MWS]

#

Doubling the sense:

Brooding over the waters
or burning in the abyss

What should and should not be

What I know and do not know.

#

What I know
is that one is called

What I do not know
is the caller

If that matters.

#

What's the matter >> why are you 'ill at ease'?
[ES]

What I know is that
in idleness or urgency

Ascending and descending
cf. Gen. 28.12
[ES]

The call descends
the response ascends

That is the matter.

#

Where do we find ourselves?
Emerson, "Experience"
[ES]

Holy: fr. OE *hálig* (whole, hale, free from injury)
Enchanted: fr. Latin, *in* + cantare (sing)
The pairing from Coleridge, natch.
[ES]

One finds oneself
in such a place

Or one finds that one
has been put in a place

Holy and enchanted.

The place of the Good above every essence is the most profound teaching, not of theology, but of philosophy.
Levinas [MH]

The text is not a mere substitute for a sanctuary or a tabernacle— it has and creates a dynamic of its own.
(Paraphrasing Moshe Idel)
[PO'L]

"Put in a place" — cf. the Aleinu, perhaps?
ve'lo samanu ke' mishpechot ha' adamah
(who has not placed us like the families of the earth …)
[ES]

REVIEWS

Passing Through: A Review of *Passing Over: Poems* by Norman Finkelstein

Henry Weinfield

"Passing Over," the long title poem of this new collection by Norman Finkelstein, the noted poet and critic, is written as a kind of descant on and accompaniment to the Passover story and ritual. Its elegiac tone and the religious/philosophical problem animating it is, however, very far removed from the spirit of the ancestral holiday. As not everyone knows or remembers, Passover derives its name from the fact that in chapter 12 of Exodus Moses tells the people that when the Lord strikes down the first born of the Egyptians he will "pass over" the houses of the Hebrews; thus the holiday celebrates our joyous deliverance not only from bondage but from death as well. In Finkelstein's poetry, however (and in this respect he speaks not only for Jewish-American poetry in general but for a crisis of modernity that continues to afflict us all), presence is always shadowed by absence, life by death, memory by oblivion, and desire by loss. For Jewish poets of Finkelstein's persuasion (the term "secular" is not entirely accurate), the source and site of presence is not God but the text; and so poetry—language—is entrusted with a memorializing function that can never express gratitude without an overlay of irony. The very title of Finkelstein's poem, "Passing Over," is elegiac in a way that the name of the Passover holiday is not: the participle applies not so much to God or the Angel of Death as to the poet and to us; it connotes a world in which everything is transient and ungrounded and in which we are all perpetual sojourners, passing over and passing through.

Tennyson called Ecclesiastes "the greatest poem of ancient or modern times." The relevance of this perspective on life and literature is far-reaching: it signifies, among other things, that the "sorrows of American-Jewish poetry"—to borrow the title of an essay of the mid-seventies by Harold Bloom—are endemic not only to American Jewish poets but to modern poets in general (Bloom, 247–62). Bloom argues that American-Jewish poetry is split between a Jewish content or vision and an American form or idiom, which cannot therefore adequately serve as its vehicle. Writing of the Objectivist poet Charles Reznikoff, for instance, he asks, "Why attempt to translate Yehudah Halevi into the idiom of Pound and William Carlos Williams?" (Bloom, 252). I happen to agree with what Bloom is saying about Reznikoff here (and am therefore in disagreement with Finkelstein himself, who, in an essay entitled "Tradition and Modernity: Charles Reznikoff and the Test of (Jewish) Poetry," takes issue with Bloom's strictures [Finkelstein, 17–34]); but it seems to me that Bloom's essay misses the larger point that Tennyson's remark reveals—i.e., that insofar as the "displaced Protestantism" (this is Bloom's term) inherent in Romantic poetic tradition increasingly embraces the kind of perspective that we find revealed in Ecclesiastes, this tradition is already in a certain crucial sense "Jewish."

Not that "American-Jewish Poetry" is a distinction without a difference (it obviously has sociological as well as historical significance), but it is certainly revealing that Finkelstein's most important poetic precursor in "Passing Over" is none other than T. S. Eliot—the Eliot of *Four Quartets*. (Eliot is not a Romantic, of course, but he too begins from the standpoint of Ecclesiastes, even as he attempts to transcend that standpoint by immersing himself in orthodox Christianity and Hinduism.) In *Four Quartets*, Eliot found a way to construct a long religious poem by varying abstract philosophical or discursive sections, in which the rhythm is a kind of loose *prosi-metrum*, with more closely-packed sections in traditional rhyme and meter. And Finkelstein in "Passing Over" does something of the same. His attempt in the poem is partly to "redeem the time" (to borrow Eliot's phrasing in "Ash Wednesday") and partly to register the fact that it cannot be redeemed. By following the way in which the Passover ritual unfolds, he wants to restore the meaning and significance that it had for him when he was a child and that it had for Jews in general prior to the crisis of modernity; but at the same time he wants to register a sense of loss that has occurred as a result of history and the passage of time. "Neither remembered nor forgotten / but remembered and forgotten / with an uncanny simultaneity," the poem's philosophical prelude begins (67), and it concludes with these lines:

> So this is a prelude
> to a ritual of remembrance
> performed around the spaces
> which oblivion has seized;
> this is an introduction
> to a thesis on forgetting,
> a study of the ways of images
> clinging to their existence.
> Its pages are interspersed
> with indecipherable signs
> and it is bound in silence,
> passed from hand to hand,
> read out at the table
> all in one night. (p. 68)

In the second section of the poem (Finkelstein avoids numbered sections, and so the poem's different movements flow into one another), the poem focuses on the images associated with the Passover ritual. The strophic writing in this second section (note the traditional use of rhyme, meter, and refrain), in my opinion, is particularly fine and effective:

> There in the corner
> and on the shelf—
> what do we search for?
> bits of ourself.
>
> *White feather, white candle,*
> *and a new wooden spoon.*

Consider this bread
as something lost.
Let us be rid of it
whatever the cost.

*Crumbs and ashes
and a few old tales.*

The day passes,
freed of desire.
Tomorrow the remnants
will feed the fire.

*White feather, white candle,
and a new wooden spoon.*

Look! the last one
behind the door.
Thus we negate,
thus we restore.

*Crumbs and ashes
and a few old tales....* (p. 69)

As "Passing Over" develops over the course of its twenty-five pages, Finkelstein makes use of many different stanzaic forms and poetic devices, all of them juxtaposed against one another and gathering significance as the poem develops against the temporal sequence of the Passover ritual. Finally, after many turnings, this strikingly ambitious and accomplished poem arrives at its own terminus by meditating on the *Chad Gadyah* ("*One kid, one kid*"), the song that concludes the Passover service, and, by doing so, at a kind of acceptance that is analogous to what one experiences in the ritual itself. In "Passing Over," however, as the poet asserts on the final page of his poem, "the Angel of Death completes the song" (p. 93). Consequently, for

Finkelstein acceptance must be of ambivalence itself:

> And if He came and killed the Angel of Death,
>   and if He came and led us to freedom,
>   what would we do in the days thereafter
>   but wonder what came next? (p. 93)

Finkelstein is an extraordinarily erudite poet, learned in many domains. His books of criticism include *The Utopian Moment in Contemporary American Poetry* (1988, 1993), *The Ritual of New Creation: Jewish Tradition and Contemporary Literature* (1992), *Not One of Them in Place: Modern Poetry and Jewish-American Identity* (2001), and *Lyrical Interference: Essays on Poetics* (2003). As a poet, he is essentially a lyric artist with a deep vein of musicality and a penchant for vatic symbolism that for many years has been anchored in Jewish thought and Jewish lore. Though Finkelstein's poetry has moved in various directions—from *The Objects in Your Life* (1976), a beautiful collection written when the poet was in his early twenties, through the three-volume *Track* project (*Track*, 1999; *Columns*, 2002; *Powers*, 2005), in which the earlier subjective, meditative mode gives way to combinatory devices and repetitive sequences—what remains consistent is the work's characteristic blend of emotional intensity and intellectuality. Finkelstein can be overly prolix and sentimental at times, and, like many contemporary American poets, even some of the finest, he does not always distinguish between his best poems and secondary efforts. At his best, however, as in some of the pieces in *Passing Over* (which was written between 1989 and 1993, by the way—that is, before Finkelstein embarked on *Track*), he can be deeply moving, in a way contemporary American poetry rarely is. *Passing Over* contains a few overwrought and even maudlin poems (I myself am quite willing to take a pass on "Mara: The Shape of an Absence," the other long sequence in the collection), but there are a number of genuinely memorable poems in this collection.

My two favorites, aside from the title poem, are "inscriptions of the body on the text" (a Finkelsteinian title, if ever there was one) and "The Oblivion of Love," a stunning meditation on D. H. Lawrence's

Women in Love, which seems to me one of the most beautiful poems in Finkelstein's oeuvre. "When Gerald comes to Gudrun in that silent house," it begins, "he knows and he does not know what he wants, / he knows and he does not know what she provides" (p. 26). This motif of knowing and not knowing is then repeated in various guises from stanza to stanza until the poem arrives at its conclusion:

> The voices follow and take up the burden
> and bear it with me for awhile. We go
> uphill, through the woods, along the banks,
> toward the source of the stream that runs
> through me and beyond. I know and I do not know
> how I came to be here: I make my way
> as the lovers make their way in the world. (pp. 26–27)

I take it that the "burden" is simultaneously a refrain (the old meaning of the word) and Wordsworth's "burthen of the mystery," but there is no straining after effect in these lines or any sense that poetic technique is on display. I love the play of "take up the burden" and "We go / uphill," the internal rhyme on "take" and "make," and the way in which the "stream" is both internal and external to the poet. The focus on self in this stanza is not narcissistic because the self is inseparable from others. In these classically balanced lines, the writing is simple, measured, and humane, pitch-perfect in its wisdom and understanding.

Works Cited

Bloom, Harold. *Figures of Capable Imagination.* New York: Continuum, 1976.

Finkelstein, Norman. *Not One of Them in Place: Modern Poetry and Jewish American Identity.* Albany, NY: SUNY Press, 2001.

The Presence and Absence of the Text: Norman Finkelstein's Recent and Early Poetry

Burt Kimmelman

Passing Over by Norman Finkelstein fills in not only a period of time in the author's life between the publication of *Restless Messengers* and the more recent *Track*, but also the evolution of his thinking, his vision, especially having to do with the power of written text to transform human self-identity; inscription is also a key to Finkelstein's identity as a Jew, a member of the people of the book. Yet, more fundamentally, writing ushers absence into the human existential equation, as Walter J. Ong and many others have shown (which helps to account for the Judaic wrestling with the deity, or potentially the cry of abandonment when God seems to have withdrawn); writing represents someone whose utterance is carried on after that person is gone. There are great implications here as regards one's conception of time but also the ontology of physicality, of space. Finkelstein's poem "Yes and No" begins,

> He is afraid to be in the presence.

> He is afraid to be in the presence of absence.

> > He is afraid, but his fear
> > breaks the backs of the sentences,
> > > suddenly understanding
> > > the journeys to Hell

[…].

It is this dynamic that forms the basis for Finkelstein's self-explanation as a human being and as a Jew.

Finkelstein's moving meditation on Judaism and his life as a Jew living in America, which constitutes the greatest part of *Passing Over*, serves as a key counterpoint to *Track*—made up of three book-length poems in a sequence, which at its deepest level involves itself in considering, again, the phenomenon of the literate human being and the possibility for spiritual sustenance. *Track* incorporates Judaic scriptural motifs among allusions to and quotes from other textual religious and literary traditions. Written prior to *Track*, but only now being published, *Passing Over* establishes an intellectual grounding for the later work and fleshes out the importance of Judaism for Finkelstein the poet. It provides possibilities for reading *Track*, which are not on the surface of the poem. *Restless Messengers* also lyrically explored Jewish identity and life. Yet in the later *Passing Over*, one written by a mature poet, there is a calm moral clarity. Consider his poem "Allegory of the Song" that begins with an allusion to Walter Benjamin's thwarted escape from the Nazis, leading to his suicide, and contains echoes of Kafka:

> At the disputed border the song is turned back.
> Denied a visa, without proper ID,
> the stateless one, begging and bluffin,
> is last seen with what little it owns,
> slumped on a bench outside a station
> in an unidentified jurisdiction.
> The stationmaster, the borderguard,
> the clerk at district headquarters,
> claim that they dealt with no such figure
>   on that particular date.

The song is at once inscribed, alive and intoned, and ephemeral. Annihilation should not disturb anyone's comfort except that the song perishes, and this death cannot ever be fully comprehended. The last stanza begins,

Think nothing of it: I was fighting off sleep
      when I came upon the scene.
    I never heard what became of it,
but it is allegory because it must be allegory,
    and the losses were tallied long ago.
Let's climb up into the hills, away from the square
where the drivers beside their trucks blow on their hands
      against an early frost.

In *Passing Over* Norman Finkelstein captures the dilemma of history and fading memory, and how, given these conditions, one might live genuinely.

Norman Finkelstein, *Track*

Peter O'Leary

1.

One of the opening sections of Norman Finkelstein's long poem *Track* runs:

> So much repetition
> in the beckoning depths
> it cannot be encompassed
>
> by parts of speech
> so that everything connects
> or nothing does.

So that everything connects or nothing does. Use this as a maxim for plying questions of the oracle of Finkelstein's poem. In essence, both amount to the same thing: either language is the great connective tissue for thought, imagination, divine intent, and human desire. Or it's not. Nevertheless, the poem—making connections or perpetuating mysteries—carries on. The section immediately following runs:

> As if poetry were epistemology
> too smart
> for their own good
>
> As if poetry were psychology
> too smart
> for my own good (14)

These two sections are a good example of the working method Finkelstein employs over the course of the three hundred pages of *Track*, a poem originally published in three separate editions beginning in 1999 with *Track*, and followed by *Columns* in 2002 and *Powers* in 2005 (all three published by Spuyten Duyvil). Namely, Finkelstein makes regular use of repetitive phrases and structures, constructing the stanzas of the brief sections that make up the poem like hinges, with one part opening one way, another part opening another way. Here's another characteristic stanza from early on in *Columns*:

> Speaking to the dead
> for the dead
>
> Speaking of speaking
> to or for the dead
>
> Speaking what was
> whispered in secret
>
> Speaking the whispers
> of or in the clouds. (107)

Each of the four stanzas begins with "Speaking." The word or functions in the second and fourth stanzas as the hinge. Speaking as a form of vocalization is paired with whispering as another form. Whispering invokes clouds, as do the dead. The section immediately following plays with these associations:

> Whispered writhe
> or wraith
>
> Whispered writhing
> wraith words
>
> Writhing wraiths
> whispered the word

Writing wraiths
whispered beauty. (107)

The pattern of the earlier section, four sets of couplets, is repeated here, as is the repetition of an opening word, "Whispered," at least for the first two stanzas. But this yields word play—from *whispered* to *writhing* to *writing*. Consider, for a moment, the tone of these samples from *Track*: it's unusual. The sections have a formulaic quality, to be sure, but the tone is one I would describe as wry earnestness. The quality of play Finkelstein explores with the repetitions, the double-takes, and the fairly straightforward language nevertheless grows with an appetite for mystical truth: there's a game he appears to be playing but there's also a Gnosis he quests after.

Came upon the combination
unlocked the words

Numbers unlocked
the words that waited

Numbers unlocked
the words that were numbers

The words that were numbered
combinations, repetitions

Numberless
words.

2.

The publication of this complete edition of *Track* by Shearsman last year provides an opportunity to assess the achievement of this poem. Finkelstein has been prolific since *Track* was first published in 1999: besides the three volumes of *Track*, he has published four additional collections of poetry: *An Assembly* in 2004, *Passing Over* in 2007,

Scribe in 2009, and *Inside the Ghost Factory* in 2010. In addition, he has published two superb works of scholarship: *Not One of Them in Place: Modern Poetry and Jewish American Identity* (2001) and *On Mount Vision: Forms of the Sacred in Contemporary American Poetry* (2010), along with a fine collection of essays, *Lyrical Interference* (2004). Each of these books could yield insight into what's happening in *Track*, but it's useful first to make a basic claim about *Track* before looking for insight. Namely, this: *Track* is *the book*. It assembles and connects all the ideas and moves that have consumed Finkelstein's poetic imagination for the past fifteen years at least. Or, to put it in terms the book provides: *Track* lays the tracks for whatever locomotion (logomotion?) operates in Finkelstein's work more largely.

So, how to think about Finkelstein's achievement in *Track?* I suggest two models: the first is to connect the poem to *On Mount Vision*, his critical study of the poetics of the sacred as seen in the works of Robert Duncan, Ronald Johnson, Jack Spicer, Susan Howe, Michael Palmer, Nathaniel Mackey, and Armand Schwerner. Track, in a sense, permitted Finkelstein to compose this study—the poem very much participates in the lineage he describes in the book. The other model I suggest is drawn from Jewish mysticism. I'm imagining a composite, chimerical model made up, in part, of elements of what the thirteenth-century Andalusian mystic Abraham Abulafia, in Gershom Scholem's *Major Trends in Jewish Mysticism*, describes as the effort "to unseal the soul, to untie the knots which bind it." Scholem refers to this practice as "ecstatic Kabbalah." The other part of this second composite model for *Track* is the Zohar, called *The Book of Radiance*, also a work of Andalusian mysticism, authored by prophetic inspiration channeled into Moses de Leon, a thirteenth-century rabbi, mystic, and Aramaic combobulator living in southern Spain. The Zohar is in essence a homiletical commentary in Aramaic on the Five Books of Moses, which are the first five books of the Bible. So, to recap, I take the two models for *Track* to be, on the one hand forms of the sacred in modern poetry; and on the other hand, the Jewish mystical interpretive techniques of ecstatic repetitions and gnostic commentary. Allow me now to elaborate slightly.

The subject of *On Mount Vision* is the American religious long poem in its more recent iterations, specifically a lineage of experimentation that emerges out of the Pound-Williams-H. D. nexus. Finkelstein begins by claiming that "the sacred remains a basic concern of poets today" (1) and furthermore that the poets on whom he focuses his attention operate with a "highly-refined and self-conscious" sense of the tradition out of which they write, which includes an awareness of the long poems that precede their own as well as "the much older and endlessly vexed tradition of sacred poetry itself" (1). Into these twining traditions, Finkelstein would clearly place *Track*. It's fair to say each of the poets he writes about has exerted an influence on his work, but some clearly more than others. Both Duncan and Johnson receive explicit homage in *Track*. Finkelstein's poem proceeds with a form of deadpan skepticism that feels indebted to Schwerner's great poem *The Tablets*. (One stanza in the poem reads, "Green beard / green Jew / the book the tablets".) But I would place Michael Palmer's work above all the rest, if only because the tone of *Track* seems so indebted to that of Palmer's work from the early 1990s. In *On Mount Vision*, as Finkelstein shrewdly observes about two lines of Palmer's poetry, "'Or maybe this / is the sacred' begins 'Untitled (September '92),' a poem in the series called Untitled.... For me, it is one of the most important moments in Palmer's entire career. What has been simmering below the surface, partially repressed, sometimes approached but more often avoided, is finally articulated. It is uttered quietly, coolly, in the typical Palmer style...." (3). I think it's fair to say Finkelstein took this moment to heart. His own poem is quiet and cool, looking effortless. "Dear J," a passage in the first volume begins:

> The inhabitants of this country

> Dear K,
> The inhabitants of this letter

> Dearest K,
> Now that you have moved to the country

> Dear T,
> You cannot be read as a journal. (58)

Besides the poets listed above, I would add the work of Joseph Donahue to this lineage. Donahue's long poem *Terra Lucida* is a gnostic complement to Track. Both poets drink from the same well.

What well? Finkelstein astutely points to Emerson's ideas, especially those in his prophetic essay "The Poet," to those who would slake their thirst for understanding why sacred poetry is so important. "All that we call sacred history attests that the birth of a poet is the principle event in chronology; poets are thus liberating gods." So says Emerson. Finkelstein elaborates, "Part of the poet's liberating power lies in his heightened awareness that 'things admit of being used as symbols, because nature is a symbol, in the whole and every part'" (8). This is the level at which for the poet *everything connects or nothing does*. The poet is a great assembler, tangler, and dissociator of symbolic correspondences. This notion plays directly into the limpid style Finkelstein devised to generate the parts of *Track*.

To this conviction, Finkelstein adds his devotion to Jewish mystical literature and its various models. Above, I mentioned ecstatic Kabbalah and the Zohar as two models from which we can draw insight into Finkelstein's poem. Ecstatic Kabbalah relies on a set of creative techniques of repetition. Two worth noting are *gematria* and *notarikon*. *Gematria* relies on Hebrew numerology. Each of the twenty-two letters of the Hebrew alphabet is ascribed a numerical value. So, for instance, the opening word of Genesis, the word *bereshit* (beginning, in the beginning, at the beginning), has a numerical value of 299. Through the practice of *gematria*, *bereshit* is thus equivalent to any other word or combination of words with the same numerical value; for instance, the Hebrew words for *gnostic*, *poison*, the *alphabet*, and even *gematria* itself (at least according to an online gematria calculator—a resource of dubious provenance but appropriate esoteric aura). *Notarikon* is similar, but involves the letters of words themselves, spun around by way of ecstatic recitation to generate novel combinations and utterances. Most famously, Abraham Abulafia generated great lists of the four letters of the Tetragrammaton, YHWH, in a great variety of combinations and orders.

Finkelstein's poem is too literary to succumb entirely to these ecstatic pronouncements. He's always ready to recast ecstasy with a cryptic eye:

> Instead of a letter
> a letter
>
> Instead of a poem
> a poem
>
> Instead of seven
> six
>
> And one. (88)

(But sometimes, ecstatic repetition will do fine, thank you very much:

> One is a book of music
> One is a spire
> One is an alphabet read backwards
> One is a bridge into the void
> One is a bridge
> One is the void
> One is a glyph that stands for void.... (131)

For the most part, as described already, Finkelstein mainly builds the parts of *Track* so that each has a hinge on which the verselets open and close; more largely, he constructs bigger hinges on which larger sections of the poem open and close. Words and themes, or anagrammic variations of words and themes, carry from one section to the next to disappear and then reappear several pages hence. One of the great pleasures of the poem is to track these appearances, to watch them come and to watch them fade.

Speaks of a garden
enclosed in a garden

A garden enclosed
within a translation.

A garden translated
from heaven to earth

A garden translated
from Greek to Hebrew. (243)

Note the subtle use of the period in this passage: it's less a mark of punctuation than a stud in the hinge.

The Zohar works less explicitly as a model for *Track* than as a kind of implicit anticipation of the poetry Finkelstein writes. After a series of preambles and parables, the Zohar begins with the "Parashat Be-Reshit," an intensive commentary on the first six books of Genesis, with a heavy attention on that opening word, *bereshit*. The word is broken down, permutated, and scrutinized to such an extent that the mythical rabbinical author of the text discovers all of creation emanating mysteriously from this opening word of scripture. Here is a characteristic moment from Daniel C. Matt's recent Pritzger translation of the Zohar: "Then this *beginning* expanded, building itself a palace worthy of glorious praise. There it sowed seed to give birth, availing worlds. The secret is: *Her stock is seed of holiness* (Isaiah 6:13)" (109-10). Worth noticing in this passage are three things relevant to understanding *Track*: in the Zohar, words have life and force of their own; the mystical vision is structured, having an architecture; and birth is a crucial metaphor. As the Zohar develops, birth gives way to arousal more generally as the great metaphor for creativity and insight.

Finkelstein shares with poet Michael Heller an admirable propensity for commentary. Both are stalwart workers in the fields of Jewish mysticism and American experimental poetry. The title of a recent poem of Heller's, "Commentary Is the Concept of Order for the Spiritual World," could serve as an axiom for Finkelstein's poetry, Track especially. (Heller took the title from a 1917 journal entry by Gershom Scholem.) In *Track*, Finkelstein brings together an architectural vision for the spiritual world (a version of what Scholem in *Major Trends of Jewish Mysticism* calls "throne mysticism," specifically, mystical writings modeled after Ezekiel's prophecy that try to envision the palace of Heaven) with a maddening proclivity for commentary, adjustment, and disputation. The work is at once visionary and literarily recombinatory. At its best, it's something altogether new: a commemoration of a poem whose whispered syllables have ceded to the perpetual motion of centuries of commentary.

> In a place where we
> may no longer write
>
> In a place about which
> we may no longer write
>
> Families of scribes
> grown into tribes
>
> Inspired
> by an absent spirit
>
>   #
>
> *Sign for "folded tent"*
> *translated as "journey"*
>
> *Sign for "sea," "tablet" and "wall"*
> *translated as "archive"*
>
> *Sign for "sky," "tablet" and "wall"*
> *translated as "temple"*
>
> *Sign for "journey"*
> *translated as "scribe."* (248)

(The pound sign—#—is used throughout the book to signal breaks in sections, sometimes doubled. It comes to represent the word "track," but also something impossible to utter as well.)

3.

Track is a major poem, written by one of the best scholar-poets in the land at the height of his powers. It's an ambitious poem, to be sure, but it wears its ambition lightly. For a poem arising out of a lineage of long poems in which difficulty is a most valued watchword, *Track* stands out for its legibility and smoothness. Even at three-hundred pages, the book reads easily. For me, it resembles H. D.'s Trilogy in this regard—one of the greatest of the American long poems. *Track* belongs in this company.

Spuyten Duyvil published the three individual volumes—a small press capable of promoting the books without much fanfare. This new Shearsman edition of the whole poem is superior on at least two counts: it's a handsomer edition of the work, smartly typeset and presented; and it collects the whole poem in one volume, affording the reader an opportunity to see the scales of the poem, both minute and vast, working their clockwork magic over the course of the volume. A tip of the hat to Shearsman for publishing *Track:* this small British press has been helping recently to keep American experimental poetry alive. We owe it a debt of gratitude.

Works Cited

Norman Finkelstein, *On Mount Vision: Forms of the Sacred in Contemporary American Poetry*, University of Iowa Press, 2010.

Norman Finkelstein, *Track*, Shearsman, 2012.

The Zohar, Pritzger Edition, volume I, translated by Daniel C. Matt, Stanford University Press, 2004.

Acknowledgments

"Lyric of Disaster / Disaster of Lyric: On Norman Finkelstein's *Track*" by Henry Weinfield first appeared as "'Two Friends': A Review of *Track* by Norman Finkelstein and *Terrible Woods: Poems 1965–2008* by Paul Bray" in *Notre Dame Review* 35 (Winter/Spring 2013), 199–211.

"Passing Through: A Review of *Passing Over: Poems* by Norman Finkelstein" by Henry Weinfield first appeared in *Shofar* 27:3. (Spring 2009), 151–55.

"A Scribe Turned into a Scribe" by Robert Archambeau first appeared in *The Offending Adam*: theoffendingadam.com/author/robertarchambeau/

Contributor Biographies

Robert Archambeau's books include the studies *Laureates and Heretics: Six Careers in American Poetry* (Notre Dame) and *Poetry and Uselessness from Coleridge to Ashbery* (Routledge); the collections of essays *The Poet Resigns: Poetry in a Difficult World* (Akron) and *Inventions of a Barbarous Age: Poetry from Conceptualism to Rhyme* (MadHat); and two volumes of poetry, *Home and Variations* (Salt) and *The Kafka Sutra* (MadHat), among others. He teaches at Lake Forest College.

Joseph Donahue's poetry collections include *Wind Maps I–VII* (Talisman House, 2019) and *Red Flash on a Black Field* (Black Square Editions, 2015), *Dark Church* (Verge Books, 2015), *Dissolves* (Talisman House, 2012), and *Terra Lucida* (Talisman House, 2009), which are sections of the ongoing poem *Terra Lucida*. He teaches in the English Department at Duke University.

Michael Heller has published over twenty-five volumes of poetry, essays, memoir and fiction. Recent books include *Constellations of Waking*, an opera libretto on Walter Benjamin, and *Telescope: Selected Poems*. A collection of essays, *Within the Inscribed*, is forthcoming in 2021.

Burt Kimmelman has published ten collections of poems as well as eight volumes of criticism and more than a hundred articles mostly on literature, some on art, architecture, and culture. He's a distinguished professor of Humanities at New Jersey Institute of Technology. Due to appear in 2021 are *Parapet: New and Selected Later Poems* (Marsh Hawk Press), *Visible at Dusk: Selected Essays of Burt Kimmelman* (Dos Madres Press), and a still untitled, edited collection of essays on the work of George Quasha.

J. Peter Moore teaches and writes on U.S. literature and culture, particularly modern and contemporary poetry and poetics, aesthetic theory and African-American literature. His book project, *Vernacular Poetics in an Era of Vernacular Studies*, examines the emergence of the term "vernacular" as an analytical category in the years following the Second World War across a number of social-scientific academic disciplines, reading this trend in relation to concurrent poetic theories of the vernacular, in an effort to explore competing ideas about the nature of informal knowledge production. He is the author of two poetry collections, *Southern Colortype* (Three Count Pour, 2013) and *Zippers and Jeans* (selva oscura, 2017).

Daniel Morris is Professor of English at Purdue.

Peter O'Leary is a poet and critic. Recent books are *Earth Is Best* (Cultural Society) and *Thick and Dazzling Darkness: Religious Poetry in a Secular Age* (Columbia). He lives in Oak Park, Illinois, and teaches at the School of the Art Institute of Chicago. With John Tipton, he edits Verge Books.

Kristen Renzi is an Associate Professor of English at Xavier University, where she teaches classes in Victorian and Transatlantic Literature, Poetry, and Theory. She is also currently the director of the Gender and Diversity Studies program at Xavier. She publishes as both a scholar and as a creative writer; recent publications include a critical book, *An Ethic of Innocence: Pragmatism, Modernity, and Women's Choice Not to Know* (SUNY UP, 2019), a poetry monograph *The God Games and Other Voices* (Main Street Rag Press, 2017).

Ariel Resnikoff is the author of *Unnatural Bird Migrator* (Operating System 2020) and the chapbooks *Ten-Four: Poems, Translations, Variations* (Operating System 2015), with Jerome Rothenberg, and *Between Shades* (Materialist Press 2014). His writing has been translated into Russian, French, Spanish, German and Hebrew. With Stephen Ross, he is at work on the first critical bilingual edition of Mikhl Likht's modernist Yiddish long poem, *Processions,* and with Lilach Lachman and Gabriel Levin, he is translating into English the collected writings of the translingual-Hebrew poet, Avot Yeshurun. Ariel has taught courses on multilingual diasporic literatures at the Center for Programs in Contemporary Writing (UPenn) and at BINA: The Jewish Movement for Social Change. In 2019, he completed his PhD in Comparative Literature and Literary Theory at the University of Pennsylvania, and he is currently a Fulbright Postdoctoral US Scholar.

Mark Scroggins is the author of five books of poetry, most recently *Pressure Dressing* and *Zion Offramp 1-50* (both from MadHat), two critical monographs, two collections of essays and reviews, and *The Poem of a Life: A Biography of Louis Zukofsky*.

Eric Murphy Selinger is the author and co-editor of several books, including (with Jonathan N. Barron) *Jewish American Poetry: Poems, Commentary, and Reflections* (Brandeis / UPNE, 2000) and, most recently, *The Routledge Research Companion to Popular Romance Fiction* (Routlege, 2020), and he has published several essays on Jewish American poets and poetry in *Parnassus*. A Professor of English at DePaul University, he has served since 2010 as the editor of the *Journal of Popular Romance Studies*.

Maeera Y. Shreiber is Associate Professor of English at the University of Utah, specializing in modern and contemporary American poetry. She is also the coeditor of two essay collections on poetry, *Dwelling in Possibility: Women Poets and Critics on Poetry* (1997) and *Mina Loy: Poet and Woman* (1997). Currently, she is working on a study of the relationships between poetry and religion.

Henry Weinfield's most recent collection of poems, *As the Crow Flies*, was published by Dos Madres Press in 2021. His translation of Pierre de Ronsard, *The Labyrinth of Love: Selected Sonnets and Other Poems*, for which he received an NEA in translation fellowship, was also published in 2021, by Parlor Press. His translation of *The Chimeras* by Gérard de Nerval, with illustrations by Douglas Kinsey, was published by Dos Madres in 2019. In addition, he edited and wrote the introduction for *From the Vast and Versal Lexicon: Selected Poems by Allen Mandelbaum*, which Pennyroyal Press published in 2018. He is Emeritus Professor of Liberal Studies and English at the University of Notre Dame, from which he retired in 2019.

Tyrone Williams teaches literature and theory at Xavier University in Cincinnati, Ohio. He is the author of several chapbooks and six books of poetry: *c.c.* (Krupskaya 2002), *On Spec* (Omnidawn 2008), *The Hero Project of the Century* (The Backwaters Press 2009), *Adventures of Pi* (Dos

Madres Press 2011), *Howell* (Atelos Books 2011) and *As Iz* (Omnidawn 2018). A limited-edition art project, *Trump l'oeil*, was published by Hostile Books in 2017. He and Jeanne Heuving edited an anthology of critical essays, *Inciting Poetics* (University of New Mexico Press, 2019). His new website is at https://www.flummoxedpoet.com/